MW00681996

UNSOLVED
MURDERS
_of_
CANADA

UNSOLVED MURDERS
of
CANADA

Lisa Wojna

QUAGMIRE
PRESS

© 2009 by Quagmire Press Ltd.
First printed in 2009 10 9 8 7 6 5 4 3 2 1
Printed in Canada

The Publisher: Quagmire Press Ltd.
Website: www.quagmirepress.com

Library and Archives Canada Cataloguing in Publication

Wojna, Lisa, 1962–
    Unsolved murders / Lisa Wojna.

ISBN 978-0-9783409-5-7

    1. Murder—Canada. 2. Murder—Investigation—Canada. I. Title.

HV6535.C3W65 2009   364.152'30971   C2009-903483-2

Project Director: Hank Boer
Project Editor: Kathy van Denderen
Cover Image: © Giorgio Fochesato | iStockphoto.com

We acknowledge the support of the Alberta Foundation for the Arts for our
publishing program.

PC: P6

Contents

Dedication

To every victim of murder, and to the loved ones they leave
behind.

Acknowledgements

Every book has a personality, and like people, some books have a way of attaching themselves to you more completely than another, and more than you could think humanly possible. This book on unsolved murders is one of those projects that managed to grip my heart like no other, absorbing many of my waking hours and invading my night dreams. Unlike the characters of a work of fiction, the people portrayed within these pages are real. They have families and friends and histories cut far too short by someone with no respect for life, and with no thought or care about the unending pain their actions would cause to so many people. It is my most earnest desire that these stories preserve the memories of these victims and serve as a warning to their killers—people are not so easily forgotten, and the murderers responsible for these deaths must know that someday they will pay for their crimes, whether it be in this life or the next.

Although it wasn't possible with every case included within these pages, I managed to contact and speak with some of the victims' family members. I'm so grateful to have met Yvonne Prior, a loving mother who has grieved the loss of her daughter, Sharron Prior, for more than three decades, and I'm also grateful for Sharron's sisters Moreen and Doreen Prior. Together, these three brave women continue to fight for justice in the rape and murder of their beloved Sharron, and they were willing to speak to me, several times over, and proof my final story despite the terrible pain that reliving those horrible memories caused. Thank you doesn't begin to express my gratitude.

A most sincere thank you also goes out to another brave woman: Denise Allan, beloved mother of Charles Horvath. Her life over the last 20 years since her son disappeared, and was later declared a victim of foul play, has been a constant quest for answers. She not only agreed to speak with me on several occasions, but she also provided me with a plethora of newspaper clippings and taped documentaries regarding her son's story. We have never met in person, but the tears we shared make me feel that I can call her a friend, and I'm so grateful for that privilege.

I owe a debt of gratitude to the many journalists who have followed these cases in the pages of their respective newspapers, to the producers, directors and broadcasters of first-rate documentaries and newscasts, and to the dedicated family members who won't sit idly by, and who actively involve themselves in the investigations surrounding the murders of their loved ones and then wrote, blogged and publicized their stories in books and websites. In particular, I'd like to acknowledge Wilma Derksen, Jake Plett, John Allore, and the Wiwcharuk family. I'd also like to acknowledge Darrin McGrath, author of *Hitching a Ride: The Unsolved Murder of Dana Bradley*.

In the preparation of this book, I was helped by several institutions that provided invaluable resource materials. Thank you to the Royal Canadian Mounted Police, various municipal and provincial police agencies, including the Calgary Police Service, the Toronto Police Service, and the Ontario Provincial Police, Sarah Ishani and the staff of Statistics Canada, the Canadian Centre for Justice Statistics, and to the researchers at the Washington State Library. A thank you also goes out to Bill Abercrombie of the Alberta Trappers' Association, to Dana Pretzer of scaredmonkeysradio.com, to Glendene Grant and all the wonderful people she sent my way, to Svea Beson for her expertise on Newfoundland and her pointers on the Dana Bradley story, to former Pointe St. Charles resident David O'Neill, to Helen Lowman at the Wetaskiwin Law Library, and as always, to the staff of the Wetaskiwin Public Library.

Thank you to my family, who are always cheering me on. Thank you to my mentor, Faye, who has allowed me the freedom to grow and the room to make mistakes. And thank you to my editor, Kathy van Denderen. Your quick eye, sharp pen and keen attention to detail has not only ironed out so many of the kinks in this book but has also helped breathe life into it.

And finally, to the staff of Quagmire Press, who allowed me the freedom to work on a book near and dear to my heart, and to the countless voices who chimed in from time to time, pointing me in the right direction for information or highlighting the flaws in my rough drafts. You all know who you are, and without your help this book would have been far less than it is today.

Introduction

Murder. The legal definition of the term, according to *Webster's Encyclopedic Unabridged Dictionary of the English Language*, is "the unlawful killing of another human being with malice aforethought." The perpetrator decided, whether it was after a lengthy contemplation and the drawing up of a detailed plan or on a sudden impulse, to take a life.

According to Statistics Canada, police reported 594 homicides in Canada in 2007. About one-third of those victims (190) were stabbed to death; roughly another third (188) were killed by the use of some sort of firearm. In urban areas, most firearms murders were committed with the use of a handgun. And in 2007, about one in five murders was gang-related.

Over the last few decades, the murder rate in Canada has been on the decline. Our country hit an all-time high, when it came to reported homicides, in the 1960s and into the early part of the 1970s. Thankfully, since around 1975, Canada has reported a slight decrease in homicides each year. Hopefully this is a trend that will continue. In the meantime, police are still busy coping with the most vicious attack one human being can commit against another—the taking of a life.

On average, investigators found that in more than 80 percent of the murders solved in 2007, the victim knew his or her killer, but that relationship is represented differently in male and female victims. In 2007, most women who were murdered were killed by someone who was close to them, such as a spouse (38 percent), family member (23 percent) or a boyfriend (5 percent). Comparative figures for male victims were 5 percent (spouse), 15 percent (family member) and 3 percent (girlfriend). In an overwhelming majority of the cases, men were murdered either by an acquaintance, a stranger or a person who the victim had some sort of criminal relationship with: 40, 20 and 18 percent respectively.

For female victims, an acquaintance is responsible for their murder about 18 percent of the time, and in about 8 percent of the cases, a criminal contact committed the homicide. Perhaps most telling is that although parents throughout the ages have warned their children to be wary of strangers, an unknown assailant was only responsible for about 8 percent of the women who were murdered.

The Royal Canadian Mounted Police (RCMP), as well as members of provincial and municipal police forces, pride themselves in solving the murders that occur in their jurisdictions. But the very real fact, and much to the chagrin of the investigators fervently examining these cases, is that many go unsolved, sometimes for decades.

In the five years between 2000 and 2004, Canadian law enforcement agencies reported a total of 2852 murders, for an average of 570.4 murders committed per year. Of that number, 2190, or 76.8 percent, were "cleared"—either charges were laid or recommended, or a sudden death previously listed as a homicide was later determined to be accidental or an act of suicide. The remaining 663, or 23.2 percent, were classified as "not cleared." In other words, an accused had not been identified and the homicide remained unsolved, leaving family and friends of these victims in a suspended sense of grief and desperate for some kind of closure.

Specifically speaking, murder alters the way people live. For example, the young children in the Wiwcharuk family of Saskatoon were instructed on ways to deal with perceived threats after 23-year-old Alexandra Wiwcharuk disappeared and was later found murdered in the spring of 1962. Alexandra's niece, Gwen Taralson, was a young girl at the time. She wrote about the fallout from that horrible period of her family's life in a document entitled "The Truth Will Set You Free," posted on Alexandra's memorial website:

> Our mother made us practice how to "SCREAM." Yes, we practiced and practiced screaming. We learned how to scream for our lives. Many times over the years, we have woken up from our dreams, still screaming. We were not allowed to walk on a sidewalk that had hedges or bushes, we had to walk in the middle of the road…

For the friends and family members of the victims portrayed in this book, and for the friends and family members of murder victims everywhere, the sudden and senseless death of a loved one haunts them endlessly. Like a chronic and unforgiving illness, the event has lingered, its effects prolonged, bringing the past into the present and future, with no resolution or relief in sight. Although these mothers and fathers and siblings have continued to live productive and giving lives, they continue to fight for justice for their loved one. They are forever defined by a single, ruthless act. And if the individual or individuals responsible for one of these murders thinks that time dulls the pain, that distance protects him or her from the effort, energy and will required to discover their names and then to follow through with the trial required to ensure a lengthy jail sentence, they couldn't be more wrong.

The Prior family persists in searching for clues, prodding memories, updating a memorial website and questioning police about the status of Sharron's case. Denise Allan is in constant contact with the RCMP in Kelowna about the disappearance of her son, Charles Horvath, in 1989—she's put everything she has into publicizing his story and keeping his memory alive.

Members of the Wiwcharuk family are actively investigating the murder of their Alexandra, speaking to the media every chance they get. Alexandra's murder is a case that has remained unsolved since 1962, and the family is determined to name a killer before the 50th anniversary of that horrible event. If that doesn't happen, another generation of Wiwcharuks are willing to step up to the plate and take over where their elders have left off.

For most of the cases featured in this book, family are unceasing in their efforts for justice, and they all believe in one universal truth—someone out there knows something about the murder of their loved one, and it's only a matter of time before that information finds its way to the authorities. Even criminals talk. They brag. They chat about their exploits with their buddies or share secrets with their lovers during pillow talk. As time passes, some of these relationships crumble and, eventually, the fear of reprisal from coming forward and dispensing information to the police diminishes among these confidants. That's what family and friends of the murdered hope for—that the "someone" who knows something will someday talk.

And what about the investigators still examining these crimes? Because answers haven't been forthcoming doesn't mean these dedicated peace officers aren't anxious about their lack of success, troubled by the faces of the murdered men and women whose families have yet to see justice served. With few exceptions—and yes, there are always exceptions—the men and women working for law and order put their heart and soul into the communities they serve. Sharron Prior's remains were discovered more than 30 years ago, and yet a cold-case officer assigned to her unsolved case a few years back told Sharron's mother that it was Sharron's face he saw every time he came in to work, every time he sat at his desk.

In November 2008, Constable Wally Henry, spokesman for the Strathcona County RCMP, spoke with Michelle Thompson of the *Edmonton Sun* about a number of murder cases that have accumulated in that area over the last several years and that remain on the books, open and unsolved.

"I think it's important to remember the human side of the investigators who investigate these crimes," he said. "Just because the public hasn't heard anything doesn't mean the files aren't being investigated. It just takes man hours and definitely the public's assistance."

This book is not a definitive resource on unsolved murder. Nor is it necessarily a comprehensive account of the unsolved murders included between these covers. Every effort has been made to acquire accurate information on each case, though it's important to note that in many cases, discrepancies exist between sources; some of the people involved have died and not every claim can be confirmed; and family members have moved away and it's not always possible to make contact. In some instances, relatives are reluctant to talk and relive what was likely one of the most painful experiences of their lives, and busy police officers weren't always able to speak freely about their investigations.

On the other hand, this book is about remembering the names and stories belonging to the murder victims included in these pages. Hopefully a story will tweak a memory. Maybe a reader will be surprised to learn of the endless pain the family members of a murder victim experiences decades after that death, and the burden of that person's knowledge will propel him or her to speak, whether it's about one of the murders profiled in this book or about another case altogether.

And at the very least, this book is about honouring the memories of people who never had the chance to live out their hopes and dreams; any errors or omissions are mine and unintentional.

Here's to hoping for justice; here's to praying for a resolution.

Chapter One

A Funeral for Christmas— Dana Bradley

A light dusting of snow had fallen on December 18, 1981, the day the Smith family motored their way from their Shea Heights residence, in St. John's, Newfoundland, along Blackhead Road and then off towards Petty Harbour-Maddox Cove. The gently falling flakes seemed more festive than the wet and rainy weather that had characterized much of that week. Still, it takes a lot more than a little rain to dampen the Christmas spirits of hardy Newfoundlanders. Grandmas and moms were busily baking fruitcakes and cakes for a Christmas Day trifle and making sure they had all the fixings for Jiggs dinner and enough peas for the pease pudding. Local radio stations were playing songs like "Grandma Got Run Over by a Reindeer," "The Mummer's Song," as well as other traditional favourites. And the malls were hectic with shoppers picking up their last-minute gifts and all the wrap and bows needed to make them into pretty packages.

With the big day just a week away, Helen and Dale Smith couldn't put off hunting for a Christmas tree any longer. The couple's youngsters were anxious to make their yearly trek and start the annual countdown to Christmas morning, and Dale knew of the perfect location for tree hunting.

Maddox Cove Road is an out-of-the-way rural thoroughfare typically devoid of human habitation, with a few exceptions: it's a great place to pick berries in the summer, to knock down a few trees and load up with firewood at any time of the year and to hunt for Christmas trees in December. The area was also a quick, 15-minute ride from the Smiths' home. Nice and convenient for a Friday afternoon outing.

Dale planned to pull over near the gravel pit—an off-ramp there was often used by youngsters as a lover's lane or a place to get away and have a few beers, so it was a well-trodden and easily accessible spot. Without too much trouble, they'd surely make it back home in plenty of time to enjoy a nice family meal together, trim the tree and maybe even put up a few decorations. The outing was also a chance to refocus on the joy that is supposed to dominate that time of year.

But a pall had been cast on the residents of St. John's that yuletide season. What the rain couldn't do to the spirits of Newfoundlanders, happenstance had.

Earlier in the week, 14-year-old Dana Bradley had simply disappeared. The spry and spirited teen was like a poster child for nice kids everywhere: sweet, well-mannered, outgoing, responsible, loved by all. She was also a teenager who, like most youngsters her age, liked to test her limits from time to time. She'd been at I.J. Samson School that Monday, and her teacher, Glenda Cluett, remembered meeting with her that afternoon and scolding her about being "on the pip" a few days earlier and forging a note from her mother, excusing her for missing classes. The scolding upset Dana so much that she'd left the meeting in tears. Chastising Dana wasn't something Cluett had to do often, and she was certain it had made an impression, and Dana wouldn't likely go on the pip again any time soon.

After school on Monday, Dana and two of her friends thumbed a ride to one girl's house on Currie Place, located a little west of the Village Mall. The trio sat around chatting about the latest music and the upcoming school dance planned for that Friday and hashing out boyfriend issues, until Penny Cobb and Dana decided it was time to make their way to Penny's house. From there, Dana called home and spoke with her grandmother. It was Dana's mother's birthday, and a special meal was planned. Dana wanted her family to know she was on her way.

By then it was nearing 5:00 PM, and although Patrick Street, where Dana and her mother, Dawn, lived, wasn't all that far away, it was probably quicker to hitch a ride than take a bus. In 1981, in the small, safe city of St. John's, hitchhiking wasn't seen as a particularly dangerous venture. Everyone did it.

That night, in a hurry to get home and without a care in the world, Dana stuck out her thumb.

Supper was ready and held up as long as possible, but Dana never showed up. Concerned, Dawn headed out to the Village Mall with a photo of her daughter. Dana and her friends often went there after school, and with Christmas a week away, maybe Dana decided to do a bit of window-shopping and simply lost track of time. When Dawn came up empty, she returned home and waited for her fiancé, Jeff Levitz. The two then started canvassing the neighbourhoods, walking the streets Dana often travelled, checking out area parks and corner stores, and showing anyone who'd take the time to look a picture of Dana. No one had seen her.

By now Dawn was frantic. It wasn't at all like Dana to be so late and nowhere to be found. Desperate for help, the couple walked into the local headquarters of the Royal Newfoundland Constabulary (RNC) to report Dana as missing. It was still too early to officially say that Dana was missing when Dawn arrived at the station—by her own account, the family had heard from Dana only a few hours earlier—and the police were apt to brush off her concern. Although they recorded the information that Dawn provided, policy dictated that they couldn't do much until the next day. And they really weren't worried.

Everyone who heard Dawn's story thought Dana was a typical youngster who was likely being a bit tardy or perhaps had a tiff with her mom or a friend and needed some time to cool off, and Dawn was just being an overly anxious mother.

Dawn knew there'd been no tiff. Missing her birthday dinner wasn't something her daughter would do unless, of course, something or someone was holding her against her will. Still, despite her convictions, all Dawn could do at this point was spend a night of worry, tossing and turning and hoping against hope that the gut-wrenching, relentless stirring she felt in the pit of her stomach was just an apprehensive mom worrying about her only child—an endearing little girl who loved to laugh and grin so much that at one point she'd tried to make it into the *Guinness Book of World Records* for holding the longest smile. As soon as she woke the next morning, Dawn once again started canvassing the neighbourhoods and making her way to I.J. Samson, the public junior high school where her daughter was finishing grade nine. Dawn checked with the teachers, Dana's friends, the woman who ran the cafeteria, the principal, with everyone she met, but the answers they provided were all the same: no one had seen Dana since Monday. Dawn returned to the police station. This time the situation was taken more seriously.

Two Constabulary officers set up a volunteer search party, and once again, the streets and stores and coffee shops where Dana had been known to frequent at one time or another were checked out. Fred Tulk, Dana's principal, was part of that initial search, and after talking to a few young people about the girl's disappearance, he learned of an old shack on the Southside Hills where teens sometimes hung out.

The information was like a ray of hope in an otherwise dark night, and searchers rushed to the location. Maybe Dana had holed up for a few days, trying to work through the ups and downs of life as a teenager. But nothing was found, and there was no sign that anyone had been in the area recently. Another night, another day, and Dana was still missing.

By Wednesday, news of Dana's disappearance had hit the local media with a vengeance. For the next three days, both *The Daily News* and *The Evening Telegram* ran stories about the missing girl, along with her picture.

And on Friday, December 18, *The Daily News* wrote an impassioned plea for information on behalf of Dana's mother, Dawn. "There's a mother in St. John's suffering the terrible agony and anguish of not knowing what happened to her daughter, only 14-years-old…" The story went on, urging anyone with any knowledge as to Dana's whereabouts to call the paper.

While Christmas lights flashed and twinkled throughout the city, it was hard for anyone to think about festive tables overflowing with food and Christmas trees lined with presents when a young girl had gone astray.

Things were about to get worse. ❧

BACK ON MADDOX COVE ROAD

As Dale Smith led his wife and kids on a leisurely stroll through the woods, likely giving his youngsters tips on how to look for fuller trees that were naturally tapered, he found himself veering off course a little. A few steps later and something in the distance caught his eye. Was it a mannequin? Funny how the absurd occurs to us in a moment of horror—thinking they'd seen a mannequin in odd places has been documented by others making similar discoveries. It's as if the human mind is pre-programmed to protect us from the truth, or the truth is so ghastly it's too dreadful for reality. After taking a step or two closer, it was painfully apparent to Dale that this was no mannequin. He'd stumbled onto the body of a young girl.

Dale later told reporters that he couldn't look at her face but noticed she was lying on her back. "I was informed after that she had books tucked up in under her arm," Smith told the CBC in 2006 on the 25th anniversary of Dana's disappearance. "Now, I never saw that because I wouldn't look that far, at her face. I didn't want that in my memory, you know." It was Dale's wife who first recognized the girl as the missing Dana Bradley.

The couple rushed their children, who were thankfully spared the experience of seeing the dead girl, back into the car. They noticed a fellow cutting wood not too far away and asked him to stay with the body while they headed back home to call 911. Within minutes of police receiving the call, three cruisers from the RNC arrived at the Smith household, and Dale guided them to Maddox Cove Road and the lifeless body of the little girl who'd captured the hearts of an entire city. ∾

A MOTHER KNOWS

Dawn Bradley knew from the very first day, when her daughter hadn't shown up for the planned birthday dinner, that something was very wrong. Dana was a typical young girl for sure: she looked for ways to skip school, she was interested in boys and she had at one time even held a party when her mother was out of town and without her mother's knowledge…until her mom found out about it later. Dana got into trouble for that lark, of course, but being scolded never caused a rift between mother and daughter. Dana wasn't unkind or unreasonable— she always knew when she deserved a reprimand.

Dana and her mother shared a bond that was more like special friends or sisters than the typical parent-child relationship. There was mutual respect, a genuine affection—Dawn's birthday celebration was an important event in Dana's life. So much so that she'd called home to say she was on her way. It made absolutely no sense that she would simply trot off on some self-made adventure.

When Dale Smith called the police that Friday, Dawn happened to be at the station. The buzz that phone call caused among the staff was a red flag to her: she knew the conversation had to have something to do with her daughter. Her first instinct was to follow the police officers, who at that point provided her with only scant information as they rushed out of the station, but after getting stopped by a red light and losing their trail, she decided to go home and, once again, call her fiancé. While she waited, Dawn could see the police cruisers through her window. They were making their way up the hill towards Shea Heights and then off into the distance.

Dawn later told reporters, "When Jeff came, we got in the car again and went in the same direction, driving around until we found them." When Dawn finally arrived at the scene, the police wouldn't let her get near the commotion, and although they wouldn't confirm they'd found her daughter, they did tell her they'd found the body of a young girl. They didn't need to say it was Dana; she knew in her heart that it was.

With more than a quarter of a century of experience in the field, Jack Lavers, chief investigator with the RCMP, under whose jurisdiction the body recovery fell, likely had some ideas about what he'd see once he arrived at Maddox Cove Road.

Murder is always most foul, especially when a helpless child is involved. But Lavers wasn't prepared for what he saw. Whoever killed Dana Bradley laid her out, fully dressed, and crossed her arms over her carefully stacked schoolbooks. At a cursory glance, it almost looked like she was sleeping in this cold, remote field, but looking at her face, and her broken jaw, shattered that image.

The scene led investigators and, later, FBI profilers, to speculate the killer had experienced some kind of remorse over what he'd done, and the way he'd left Dana indicated some sort of belated respect for the body. It's a common theory applied to unidentified suspects who stage the scene surrounding a body recovery site in this way. Then again, as criminologist Dr. Elliott Leyton would later point out, the action could have been nothing more than "just good old psychopathic obsessive-compulsion."

Reporter Mike Harris would have most likely agreed with the latter parallel. In 1999, he reflected on the story he had covered so closely and for so long, melding the experience into an opinion column for *The Ottawa Sun*. Harris was focusing on a more recent murder, the response of the Canadian justice system to that crime, and comparing it to the Dana Bradley case. In the article, he called the suggestion that Dana's killer showed any remorse so absurd that the "thought makes me dizzy to this day…The person who smashed in Dana's beautiful head also forced plugs of soil into her nostrils to make sure that she died." It was many years before the general public would learn of that detail. At the time that Dana Bradley's body was discovered, all the police were saying was that they didn't think she had died of natural causes. An autopsy was scheduled for 9:00 AM on Saturday, December 19.

Meanwhile, the community of St. John's didn't need an official statement from the police or a story in the media to know the basics about what was going on. More than half a dozen marked and unmarked police cruisers were on Maddox Cove Road at any given time on the evening of December 18, and a good portion of the city could see from their front porch that something was brewing.

While reporters and photographers from St. John's dailies were arriving at the scene, gathering the details of the discovery for the morning papers, people in town were already talking. Dana's teacher, Glenda Cluett, didn't even need to turn on her radio or television to hear the news: she learned that Dana had been found dead from an acquaintance she'd passed while doing some errands along Water Street.

Even in the midst of horror, life goes on. By 7:00 PM that Friday night, the doors of I.J. Sampson were about to open for the dance that Dana had excitedly talked about with her friends a few days earlier. The police had already called school principal Fred Tulk with the basics surrounding the discovery and their belief that the body they'd found was that of the missing girl, and for a moment Fred considered cancelling the dance. But at a time when school counsellors and grief therapists weren't readily available for such an unthinkable tragedy, Tulk thought the event might hold some therapeutic value for the staff and students alike. Gathering together all the teachers and volunteer parents he could, Tulk opened the school doors and prepared for the difficult night ahead.

Not a single student took to the dance floor. Instead of the boys and girls lining up on either side of the school gymnasium, daring each other to venture out and grab a partner, they huddled together in small groups. The usual laughter and teasing of dance night was replaced with tears. The teens cried on each other's shoulders.

Parents and teachers tried to comfort the youngsters as well as they could, but as more information about Dana's death was released during regular television and radio updates, and as more residents learned the young girl was found murdered, the fear level among the students rose. Even young people attending other schools, kids who didn't grow up with or have anything to do with Dana, were traumatized.

"It just seemed to me that it was everywhere. Every time you turned on the TV, or the radio, it was all you heard," explains Svea Beson, who was also 14 and lived in St. John's when Dana Bradley was murdered. Looking back, she remembers the constant murmur in coffee shops and in the mall. People who once gathered to complain about the weather or the commercialization of Christmas were now talking about the horrible crime committed against one of their youth. "It was just everywhere. Even just walking down the street, you'd hear people talking about it...that it was all anybody talked about...my friends... everybody."

On Saturday morning, the papers led with the breaking news. If the Dana Bradley story hadn't monopolized the media to that point, it certainly would for the foreseeable future. Most people, although they were unquestionably worried about the missing girl all along, surely hadn't expected this.

Dana's teacher had worried that maybe her reprimand so upset the girl that she'd run away. Some of the townsfolk thought that perhaps the girl had been abducted for some reason. There were even whispers that she'd gotten herself pregnant and took off to have the baby somewhere else. And although Dawn and her fiancé Jeff were worried, they certainly didn't see this coming. "There was no thought that she might end up not living through the ordeal," Jeff told a CTV News documentary in 2003.

Collectively, the city of St. John's also hadn't expected they'd have a murder on their hands. The city has a reputation for maintaining one of the lowest crime rates in the country. And any murders that had occurred to that point were, with a few exceptions, solved in a timely manner. Following the typical chain of events in the majority of murder cases, a murder victim usually knows his or her attacker. Discover that kind of link, and investigators have a starting point when it comes to uncovering method and motive, unearthing evidence and eventually apprehending and imprisoning a killer.

Dana Bradley's murder was different. In relatively short order, everyone who knew the young girl—friends, family members and even distant acquaintances—were questioned and ruled out as suspects. That left police with the realization that Dana's murder was the result of a random act of violence, or at the very least a violent act planned and carried out by a stranger.

With no known relationship between victim and perpetrator, investigators would have an infinitely more difficult time honing in on the person or persons responsible for Dana's death: it was also a motivating factor in the aggressive way police kept the public informed and encouraged tips through regular media updates. Besides, if this was a stranger abduction, it wasn't disturbing news just for Dana's family and friends and investigators working the case. It would forever change the overall feeling of safety that residents of St. John's previously felt, and it would challenge all levels of the province's law enforcement like it had never been challenged before.

ENTREPRENEURS COME FORWARD

Police had their first real lead into what might have happened to Dana Bradley on Wednesday, December 16, after her photo ran in the local newspapers. John and Harry Smeaton were trying their hand at a new money-making venture that December. The brothers had set up shop in an empty lot on Topsail Road, across from a busy McDonald's restaurant. The pair was selling Christmas trees to bring in a little extra cash for the holiday season. Sales were a lot lower than they'd expected, and the brothers, feeling somewhat discouraged and getting increasingly chilled, decided to sit in their truck for a while to warm up.

"We were sitting in the truck commenting on people passing by, and we commented on this little girl who was hitchhiking," Harry told Darrin McGrath, author of *Hitching a Ride: The Unsolved Murder of Dana Bradley*. The brothers thought maybe the girl was originally waiting for a bus but then got a little impatient when one didn't happen along and, instead, decided to thumb a ride. Although it was getting dark, they could see that Dana was standing by a bus stop, and when a car finally stopped, the nearby streetlight gave the brothers a chance to get a good look at the vehicle and at the driver.

Dana tried to open the passenger door, but it was stuck. Harry remembered that the driver had leaned across the front seat to open the door from the inside. The glow of the streetlight had illuminated the driver's face, giving the brothers a clear view of the man who they described as clean-shaven, 20-something and pretty much average in the height and weight categories. They also remembered his hair as being "light-brown, medium-length" and "unkempt." From the Smeatons' depiction of the driver, it's understandable that young Dana may not have perceived any threat. Like most feisty 14-year-olds, Dana was pretty confident she could defend herself. He looked harmless enough. But who was this unknown man?

Despite the fact that the Smeatons called the RNC the Wednesday that Dana's picture first appeared in the newspaper, it wasn't until after Dana's body was discovered that members of the Constabulary, along with officers from the RCMP, interviewed the brothers about the incident.

Although Dana's disappearance took place in St. John's, where the RNC has jurisdiction, because her body was found outside the city meant the RCMP would also work on the case. From the time her body was discovered, the investigation involved a joint task force made up of sometimes more than two-dozen members from both forces at any one time. And the man at the helm was Chief Investigator Jack Lavers.

Using the Smeatons' description, Lavers instructed a police sketch artist to develop a composite of the man. It was a start, but the Smeatons had more to offer the police. They'd taken particular notice of the car that Dana got into—had it narrowed down to either a Dodge Dart or Plymouth Valiant, and either yellow, beige or a pea green in colour, not unlike the shade of pease pudding. The brothers remembered the car was a four-door variety, that the lower part of the body was riddled with rust, and they even remembered a partial licence plate number. Using this eyewitness information, investigators narrowed down the model of the vehicle to one that would have rolled off the production line sometime between 1973 and 1976.

If the police had any concerns about the accuracy of information provided by the entrepreneurial brothers, they didn't have to worry for long. Soon after, a truck driver called the police to say that he remembered seeing a young girl who looked like the newspaper photo of Dana at that same location along Topsail Road. The truck driver also described how she leaned into the car under a street lamp, and his description of the vehicle was similar to the one provided by the Smeatons.

Armed now with two descriptions of a suspect and a car, police were likely hoping to make up for lost time. Dana had been missing for four days before she was discovered. That gave the killer a significant head start. But if he wasn't worried about being caught up to that point, learning that the suspect and vehicle descriptions were released in the St. John's dailies for all to see must have given him some pause for concern.

Almost as soon as the papers hit the newsstands, phones at the Constabulary started to ring. People wanted to help in whatever capacity they could and, as it turned out, everybody knew someone with a car matching the Smeatons' description. From December 20 to December 31, the police scrutinized as many as 72 cars per day—more than 800 Plymouth/ Dodge combinations rolled past the fine-tuned analysis of investigators. Reflecting on the experience, Officer Randy Hogg said, "It seemed like everybody had [the kind of car they were looking for] and every single one had rust along the bottom." Despite a dedicated effort, the police had yet to find the right car. But they were far from ready to give up looking.

Even though residents were great about providing tips, one has to expect that a killer isn't going to volunteer his car for inspection. A savvy criminal could have sold it or ditched it. The first step in searching for cars that weren't brought in voluntarily meant officers had to cull through motor vehicle records to find cars fitting witness descriptions of possible makes and models. But nothing is ever as straightforward as it seems. Even with a partial licence plate number to work with, the police found themselves up against unforeseen roadblocks. Incomplete registrations listed some Dodge Darts as simply "Dodge," or some Plymouth Valiants as "Plymouth," and to complicate matters, the province had started changing all numbered licence plates to a letter-number combination earlier that year. Sorting through the information seemed like an insurmountable task.

Still, investigators were persistent. Police were diligent in keeping their eyes open for places where someone might have dumped a car. The geography of Newfoundland resembles a big empty forest where, every now and then, a town is thrown in— there is no shortage of potential dumpsites. At one point, a car, discovered in a location that was both remote and almost impossible to retrieve, had to be raised by a helicopter before it could be searched for evidence. Hogg told McGrath that investigators went "through that car with a fine-tooth comb. We thought for sure we had the car, but we just couldn't find anything."

Another glitch presented itself in the early days of the investigation in the form of witness accounts of a man picking up females along Topsail Road. Several young girls, frightened by what happened to Dana, were coming forward and telling police about their experiences, but their collective description of the individual they took their rides from differed from the description provided by the Smeatons. And yet despite these differences, police had to take the complaints seriously, and considerable manpower was expended in an effort to find and question that individual.

"It took us about three to four days to apprehend that person," Lavers said. "We found out that the person was not the [suspect in the Bradley case], but he was active in picking up young girls in that particular part of town. So there was some delay and confusion in terms of composite drawings and things of that nature." ∾

CAUSE OF DEATH

While the media continued to cover the investigation, and police worked their way through a barrage of phone tips daily, what exactly had happened to young Dana—and how she died—remained a bit of a mystery. Police were understandably tight-lipped about the details, not wanting to jeopardize their investigation.

On Monday, December 21, *The Daily News* and *The Evening Telegram* reported on the results of Dana's autopsy. It was ruled that the cause of death was severe blows to the head. There was no mention of any kind of sexual assault, and the absence of that kind of confirmation led most folks to the logical question of why she was killed in the first place. She wasn't wandering around with a lot of money in her pocket. She wasn't into the hardcore drug scene. She was too young to provoke some kind of rage attack from an ex-lover. Aside from her funeral notice, in which her family asked that "in lieu of flowers, donations could be made to the Rape Crisis Centre in St. John's," mention of a sexual assault didn't appear in the media until many years later.

It really didn't matter. Whether it came down through the official channels or not, the rumble through town was that young Dana Bradley had to have been a victim of a sex crime.

Although there is often truth behind some rumours, others are perpetuated by fear. Svea Beson remembers talk about another body being found when officers were searching Maddox Cove Road after finding Dana's remains and while they were looking for evidence, and that there might be a serial killer on the loose. Given the area's history, which in reality wasn't as complete a stranger to crime as residents may have liked to believe, it was understandable.

Three years earlier, also in December, 17-year-old Sharon Drover disappeared during what most thought at the time to be a trip to pick up her paycheque at the Kenmount Road McDonald's in St. John's. It was more than 10 years before two brothers responded to a news report with an update on the story.

The brothers told police that they'd picked up a hitchhiker fitting Sharon's description on Kenmount Road on the night in question and had dropped her off close to her boarding home. They thought they'd seen her talking to a man in front of her house and then running away. Again, police spent considerable manpower investigating the tip but came up empty. Sharon Drover's body has never been found.

A few months after Sharon's disappearance, on February 6, 1979, 16-year-old Janet Louvelle also went missing. In June of that year, her partially nude body was discovered in a wooded area about 12 kilometres from Corner Brook. She'd been stabbed.

Although Malcolm Norman Cuff pled guilty to the manslaughter death of Louvelle on January 31, 2000, more than 22 years after her death, at the time of Dana Bradley's murder, the Drover and Louvelle cases were still unsolved. So in the minds of residents, it made perfect sense to think that a serial killer might be roaming the otherwise safe streets of Newfoundland's neighbourhoods—it was inconceivable to think that three different people were responsible for the three crimes.

As well as working the Bradley case, police were now also faced with the need to reassure area residents that they needn't be looking over their shoulders in paranoia. Although investigators later admitted that they had thoroughly looked at these and other unsolved crimes in light of the Dana Bradley case, Inspector Jack Lavers publicly squelched the rumours of a serial killer, and police got on with their investigation.

Family and friends, meanwhile, got on with the business of grieving the loss of the young girl who'd brought so much joy into their lives. Dana Bradley's funeral was held on Monday, December 21. During the morning, staff at I.J. Samson supported their students through an in-school assembly conducted by the school chaplain. The school closed at noon, and many of the students made their way to Wesley United Church, located on the same street Dana once called home, and braced themselves for her funeral.

The standing-room-only crowd was overwhelmed with emotion—it was all the six young men carrying Dana's casket could do to make it to her graveside in the Mount Pleasant Cemetery before breaking down with emotion.

Dawn Bradley was so overwhelmed with grief she couldn't attend her own daughter's service. To add to her pain, pranksters repeatedly called the Bradley household, asking to speak to the dead girl or outright claiming responsibility in her death. One individual in particular was so persistent that police spent considerable time tracking him down, thinking that perhaps the deranged caller was Dana's murderer. Bruce Gerard Connors was eventually apprehended. He was cleared of any responsibility in Dana's murder but was charged with public mischief. He was sentenced to nine months in jail.

Christmas was looming, more like a cloud than the festival of lights it is meant to be, but people still found time to call in tips on the Bradley case. The police were still wading their way through vehicle records: they'd eventually inspect more than 2000 vehicles matching the initial witness descriptions of the car before every one of them was ruled out as the suspect's vehicle.

And then during that week before Christmas, a couple of rather interesting twists occurred in the investigation. Several witnesses came forward to say they'd seen another man, this one in his mid to late 20s, with shaggy, brown hair, a moustache, and wearing tinted glasses in the vicinity of Maddox Cove Road over a two-and-a-half-hour period the day before Dana's body was discovered. This individual was reportedly driving a green four-door Chevy sedan, 1973 model, and although investigators hadn't seriously considered that Dana's killer had an accomplice, the information demanded their attention.

Perhaps even more telling was the story from a couple who lived in the Shea Heights area of St. John's. The two, who wanted to remain anonymous to the media, said that on the day Dana went missing, they were driving along Maddox Cove Road around 11:30 PM, and they remembered noticing a car parked near where Dana's body was recovered. They also recalled that the passenger door was open and the interior light revealed the car's beige interior. About 4.5 metres away, they said they saw the figure of a man. They thought nothing of it at the time—we've all been caught by the call of nature at one time or another, and it was quite possible the gent was stopping to relieve himself. But after Dana's body was discovered, the couple realized they could have witnessed the murderer dumping her small, frail body.

These new witnesses also provided police with a description of the man—and he bore a striking resemblance to the earlier descriptions of the person who'd stopped to pick up Dana on Topsail Road. The information led investigators to develop the theory that the couple had indeed spotted the murderer, or at the very least the individual who'd placed Dana's body at the Maddox Cove Road dumpsite. It would certainly explain why there appeared to be no effort to hide Dana's remains.

As Jack Lavers pointed out, "There was no debris, or brush, or rocks or grass or any effort made to conceal the body... there was a fender or a hood of a vehicle very close to where the body was found, and there was no effort made to cover the body up with this large piece of metal." Noticing the car, the man in the bushes likely panicked. He had good reason to panic. If he read the papers over the next few days, he would have learned that he'd been seen not just on Topsail Road, but on Maddox Cove Road as well.

Christmas Eve brought with it the horrible news that there could be two men involved in Dana's murder. Both papers ran stories about the two potential suspects, and police were working around the clock trying to solve the murder before Christmas. None of the police officers working the case slept, save for a few short hours a day. Calls kept coming in. And the mood throughout St. John's was as dreary as the weather.

An arrest before Christmas was not to be. The big day came and went, and the investigation appeared to most residents to have stalled. As many as 250 suspects had been questioned and polygraphed. Police also took hair samples from several of the suspects by then, but still nothing. At one point they apprehended a man in Kilbride for questioning. He had at one time owned a car that fit the description of the suspect's vehicle, but he was released after passing a polygraph test. ∾

MIXED MEMORIES

At this point in the investigation, Staff-Sergeant Pat Dunleavy of the Criminal Identification Branch in Ottawa made his way to St. John's to offer his expertise. Dunleavy, an expert in the field of composite drawings, set out to re-interview witnesses and, using a technique he developed that drew on a library of different eye, ear, mouth, nose and chin templates, constructed another composite drawing. The plan was to run the updated sketch of the suspect if the witnesses felt Dunleavy's methods got them a little closer to the man they remembered. His efforts met with mixed results. Everyone remembered things a little differently, and even though the two sketches were again published in the local media, Dunleavy cautioned the public that the new sketch was still only a likeness, not a photographic replica of the suspect.

Descriptions of the car also altered slightly as new information came forward. In particular, there seemed to be a discrepancy between witnesses on the colour of the car. Police were now looking for a car that was tan or faded yellow or lime green. Of course, evening falls early at that time of year in St. John's, and darkness has a tendency to distort the details. Police attributed the discrepancies surrounding the car's colour on various lighting conditions. Still, they had to consider all the possibilities, and that meant even more cars had to be examined.

In March 1982, the investigation into Dana's murder broadened beyond the confines of the island, venturing into two

cities that were long-time favourite destinations for Newfoundlanders searching out new and exciting work opportunities:
Toronto, Ontario, and Fort McMurray, Alberta. Throughout
the year, the search even broadened into the United States, and
persons of interest were interviewed in every Canadian province
except PEI and Saskatchewan.

Then on December 10, 1982, four days before the first
anniversary of Dana's disappearance, another woman went
missing from St. John's. Twenty-five-year-old Henrietta Mille
had a child in foster care and was planning to visit her little one
when she vanished from The Key Club. Her purse and personal
items were recovered at the bar, but Henrietta was never seen or
heard from again. A few days later, an anniversary story of
Dana's disappearance and murder ran in the local papers. Even
then, a year later, people were talking about the murdered girl,
and tips were still flowing into the police, but with yet another
missing woman in their midst, talk of a serial killer once again
reared its ugly head whenever folks gathered over a cup of tea. It
was a long time before anything that looked like a break in the
case was forthcoming. Two years later, in 1984, another woman,
20-year-old Pamela Asprey, went missing from St. John's. What
was happening in this safe, low-crime city? ∾

SUSPECT APPREHENDED

He was already in custody and was getting ready to
make his first court appearance when residents of St. John's

learned that at long last, an arrest had been made in Dana Bradley's murder. On January 24, 1986, more than four years after
her death, both of the St. John's dailies carried the story
announcing the arrest. The news item ran with Dunleavy's
re-creation of the earlier composite drawing, but folks had yet to
see a photograph, a real picture, of the man. Even with such
short notice, St. John's provincial court was full of spectators
waiting to catch a glimpse of the alleged killer.

By now, David Somerton was 35 years old, but he still
bore a striking resemblance to earlier witness descriptions. He
was average in almost every respect: 5 feet, 8 inches tall, with
short, light brown hair, moustache and goatee. A news story
explained that Somerton was apprehended at his Jersey Avenue
home in the neighbourhood of Mount Pearl, where he lived,
quietly and unpretentiously, with a woman. Somerton's defence
attorney, Robert Simmonds, asked for a publication ban on the
case, and Judge John Trahey agreed to impose one.

The court proceedings may have been out of bounds for
reporters, but writing about what the police were up to while
Somerton was facing his charges was not. Maddox Cove Road
was a flurry of activity, as was the St. John's dump. A team of
about a dozen Mounties led by RCMP Staff-Sergeant Penney
cordoned off an area stretching about 395 metres along the
Maddox Cove roadway and 38 metres into the woods. Investigators were equipped with pickaxes, shovels and chainsaws to
help them clear the area in search of some potential evidence.

All Penney could tell reporters was that they were "looking for material evidence that might support a criminal investigation." Nobody bought that explanation. The talk of the town was that police were looking for a murder weapon.

Officers were also starting to dig up the dump, excavating the tons of concrete discarded there when the Hotel Newfoundland was demolished. The only thing officers would say to the media about the beehive of activity was that they were looking for "evidence." But more than 300 abandoned vehicles were underneath all the rubble, and with the sudden urgency on the part of the investigators, folks in St. John's were pretty sure the cops were looking to examine each and every car that in any way resembled the one that Dana Bradley was supposed to have gotten into. The problem was in getting at them.

Although figuring out what the officers were up to didn't take a huge stretch of the imagination, no one had a clue why police had arrested Somerton. Sure, he was a bit of an odd duck, but a murderer? The conundrum kept coffee shops humming long after charges against Somerton were eventually stayed. Whatever the cops were digging for, those crucial pieces of evidence that "might support a criminal investigation," weren't there—or at least they couldn't find them. Four years had passed since the car that police were so desperate to find had been dumped in the landfill, so even if investigators were lucky enough to get their hands on the right vehicle, any evidence that might have been inside it would have likely been destroyed by the elements.

And the search of Maddox Cove Road didn't yield what folks would later learn was the weapon that Somerton said he had killed Dana Bradley with: a "blackjack which is a lead-weighted weapon on one end, with a spring handle." The police hadn't been able to find the material evidence they were looking for, and an official announcement eventually came through the office of the Minister of Justice: "The Crown has decided, following a costly and intensive police investigation into the December 1981 death of 14-year-old Dana Bradley, to place a stay of proceedings on a first-degree murder charge against David Grant Somerton, charged three months ago in connection with the teenager's death."

The reason for Somerton's arrest came out in McGrath's book, which was published in 2003. That's when the public learned that prior to their search of Somerton's home in 1986, the police had found a handwritten note that fingered Somerton for Dana's murder. The strange thing was that when officers raised the indented information written on the page underneath the note, by using a pencil to shade the indented portion, they came up with numbers that were eventually traced back to a prescription belonging to Somerton. A handwriting analysis confirmed the identity of the writer: the person pointing the police in Somerton's direction was none other than Somerton himself.

The note in itself might not have been enough to arrest Somerton, but it got him into an interrogation room, and it was only a matter of time before he made a full confession. It was details provided through Somerton's confession that turned police loose on the old dump, and it was Somerton who told police that the weapon used to bludgeon Dana Bradley was somewhere on that desolate, Maddox Cove Road hillside.

Somerton was charged with murder and, following his first court appearance, he was remanded in custody. After his second appearance, he was sent for a 30-day psychiatric assessment at St. John's Waterford Hospital. The assessment would determine his fitness to stand trial, and as it turned out, he received the green light. Somerton was not crazy—at least not clinically. But folks had to wonder about that judgement when Somerton recanted his confession. What motivates a sane person to turn himself in and confess in great detail to a grizzly crime, only to later rebut his own words?

Still, the fact remained that without the car and the murder weapon, the police had no physical evidence to tie Somerton to the crime. Rather than take a chance of losing in court, therefore abandoning any hope of a conviction, Crown prosecutor Bernard Coffey entered the stay of proceedings. That would, in effect, give investigators one year to find the physical evidence they were so desperate to locate, thereby going to trial with an airtight case instead of one that could be lost through "reasonable doubt."

Somerton didn't get off altogether, though. He wrote the original note, a fact that was corroborated by the handwriting analysis, so at the very least, he was guilty of public mischief. Coffey asked Judge Joseph Woodrow to impose the maximum 10-year sentence, but defence attorney Simmonds played the pity card, saying Somerton had had a rough childhood in which he was placed in one inadequate foster home after another, and the defendant was currently trying to work out a number of personal problems with his psychiatrist. Simmonds also explained that although Somerton had five priors on his rap sheet, including one for robbery, Somerton had worked hard over the last six years and made "valiant efforts towards rehabilitation." Judge Woodrow took Simmonds' comments into consideration but still slammed Somerton with a two-year sentence for public mischief. After all, Somerton's make-believe confession had cost Newfoundland taxpayers more than a million dollars for the excavation of the dump and the Maddox Cove Road site alone.

During a documentary presentation in 2003 of the Dana Bradley murder, CTV News asked Somerton why he originally confessed to the crime. In a word, he said he was overwhelmed. "After being there [under police interrogation] for 18 hours, and I knew that I was flipping out on them and on myself because I was in a suicidal state in that room…I was doing anything to get them off my back to make it out of that room…including confessing. I've been regretting it ever since." One has to wonder why, then, he wrote the original note that effectively set the course of his life for the last three decades.

Investigators, on the other hand, still questioned whether Somerton had been telling the truth the first time around. "A team of two senior investigators did the interrogation, and I observed most of the interrogation through a one-way glass," Lavers later explained. "He [Somerton] was quite convincing in the fact he gave a statement that he was able to describe how he killed Dana Bradley, what weapon he used, where he did it, how he did it and when he did it. And there were certain things within his statement that we had not released to the public and we didn't expect that he would know." ∾

A LOOK BACK

After Somerton spent time in jail for his public mischief charge, one might expect he would have been extra careful not to get into any legal predicaments. But in 1996, he was again in trouble with the law, charged and convicted of assaulting a teenage girl, and in 1999, he pled guilty to yet another sexual assault involving a minor, although not before a SWAT team flushed him out of a home in Calgary in August of that year. And in the midst of it all, he still hadn't seen the end of the Dana Bradley case.

The province of Newfoundland and Labrador is home to roughly 505,000 residents. Although the land is vast, communities are close, folks look out for one another and no amount of time passing could erase thoughts of Dana Bradley. Tips still came in to the investigators working the now long-cold case, but everyone involved couldn't help but feel a little discouraged that the brutal murder hadn't been solved.

And then, in 1991, the investigation got an infusion of energy with a $10,000 reward for information leading to an arrest and conviction in the case. A re-enactment of Dana's disappearance and murder was televised in the hope that it would spark people's memory, and it did. Police responded to about 200 new tips. On December 4, 1992, the murder was again featured, this time as a Crime Stoppers "unsolved crime of the week." Crime Stoppers was newly established in Newfoundland, and the Bradley case was one of its first priorities. A reward of $1000 was offered this time, again for information leading to an arrest and conviction, and once again folks called in with new tips.

By 1993, officers were still keen on David Somerton as a person of interest in the case, but after culling through as many as 1800 persons of interest, they narrowed the focus down to three or four individuals. Officers were once again considering the possibility that more than one person was responsible for Dana Bradley's murder, and a team of five Alberta RCMP officers questioned several individuals in that province, all of whom were former Newfoundlanders working in Alberta's oil patch, but only one was considered a key suspect.

At this point, Lavers had long since retired from the RCMP and now hung his shingle as a lawyer, so the Bradley file had passed through several hands. In December 1993, Sergeant

Keith McGuire was the lead investigator, and he travelled to Edmonton for nine days of interviews with the key person of interest as well as several potential witnesses in the case. "I can't say that we're confident that we're going to make an arrest, and I can't say that we're confident that this is going to be solved," McGuire told the media in 1993. "At some time, I'd say that somebody will have to make a decision on what we can do with that information, but for right now we're just continuing to investigate the homicide."

There was no arrest made in 1993 or the following year. But by March 1995, the investigation was once again heating up on several fronts. Details of the case had been entered into the Violent Crime Linkage Analysis System (ViCLAS). Before ViCLAS, police departments primarily operated independently of one another. The newly established national database allowed law enforcement personnel to share information across jurisdictions. That way, if, for example, a suspected serial killer has victims in several provinces, similarities in the case could be pinpointed, information shared and efforts between departments organized.

Police searched Somerton's St. John's home again that year, and items of interest to the case were collected. They also took blood samples from Somerton and from the Alberta suspect, who was described in McGrath's book as "less than 30 years old and [working] at an Alberta printing company." Both suspects underwent a polygraph test. Media reports in

1993 suggested a charge would be forthcoming that year, and said the same thing again in June 1994, but nothing concrete had been filed against the investigators' lead suspect in the case, David Somerton. Nor had charges been filed against anyone police had questioned in Alberta or any other person of interest in the case. But police weren't letting up. ∽

LOOKING TO SCIENCE

There was still news to be made, however. It was during this segment of the investigation, more than a decade after Dana Bradley's murder, that the public first learned that "foreign scalp and pubic hair" samples had been discovered at the site where Dana's body was found. The samples were small, only 10 scant hairs, and in 1981, any kind of detailed testing would have destroyed the evidence. Only cursory tests were allowed, but new advances in DNA technology were on the horizon.

In 2000, Constable Christine MacNaughton personally delivered the hair samples to LabCore Mitochondria DNA Laboratory in Raleigh, North Carolina. MacNaughton had taken over the reins as lead investigator by then and was hoping the new technology could produce a DNA profile from the rootless or partial hair samples from the Bradley case—before this procedure was perfected, a root was required to establish a DNA profile. Although a positive match wouldn't get a slam-dunk for the prosecution, it could get them a lot closer to putting away the killer or killers who'd been eluding capture for so long. Unfortunately, the mitochondrial DNA testing didn't provide investigators with a match.

Almost three decades have passed since Dawn Bradley buried her only child—and charges have yet to be laid against anyone. But Dana's file isn't sitting on a shelf somewhere, gathering dust. "This is not an investigation that's been put to the side," RCMP Sergeant Pete McKay told reporters from *The Evening Telegram* in 2006. "It has always been active. We're just waiting for someone to come forward with more information."

People in St. John's don't always talk about Dana Bradley, but her name comes up from time to time. Whenever someone goes missing or there's been a murder, the memory of that sad Christmas all those years ago isn't far away. Young Dana Bradley became a daughter to an entire province. Everyone cared in 1981. They still care today. And that is a powerful tool when it comes to catching a criminal. Because even if the killer dies before he's put behind bars, as happened to one suspect who was living in Vancouver at the time, Dana Bradley's murderer has never really known what it's like to be free—he has been looking over his shoulder all his life.

Chapter Two

Stolen Innocence—Sharron Prior

The sonorous yaw of a hand accordion meters out the sounds of a traditional Irish folk tune, drawing crowds and curious passersby in the Montréal neighbourhood of Pointe St. Charles, Québec. Men in dark coats tip their hats to women sashaying across the park grounds in long, lace-busted dresses. And the scene unfolds, spelling out a chapter of Canada's history from the first days of this industrial, working-class community nestled along the Old Montréal Harbour, a little more than a stone's throw from the more affluent communities in other parts of the city. Children clamour for hot dogs and candy apples, as children will do, and the good warm feelings of family and friends getting together for a bit of old-fashioned fun is enough to drive away the sting of fall, drifting in off the nearby St. Lawrence River. If you find yourself driving through the neighbourhood one sunny day in September and happen across just such a scene, you've found your way to the Pointe Saint-Charles Heritage Days celebration.

Folks in Pointe St. Charles have always mingled together. Historically, the community is composed of a variety of cultural groups, but it's the Irish—as many as 30,000 each year in the 1800s—who make up one of the largest segments of the ethnic population. Immigrants from England and Scotland, and the French as well, added to the mosaic that came to be known as "The Point," a neighbourhood in the Montréal borough of Le Sud-Ouest. The strong work ethic these immigrants brought to the area helped them form durable bonds with one another; neighbours lonely for friends and family in the old country were anxious to get to know each other, and, pretty soon, many who lived at The Point saw themselves as one big happy family.

By the mid 1900s, that family atmosphere was still strongly evident. It's one of the things that attracted Yvonne Prior to the area. Born in England, Yvonne was nine years old when her parents immigrated to Montréal in 1946. As a young adult, Yvonne chose to live in The Point. It's where she met her husband, George, and in 1959, the couple welcomed their first child, a daughter named Sharron, into the world. Two years later, the couple was doubly blessed with the birth of twin girls, Moreen and Doreen. Yvonne was sad to leave The Point when, in 1962, her husband, a private in the Canadian army, was transferred to Brandon, Manitoba. That's where the couple completed their family with the birth of a son, George Jr. But in 1965, Yvonne and her husband separated, and it didn't take long for her to decide what to do—she moved back to The Point.

"My mother and other family were still here…Where we lived on Congregation Street, there were families with 10 and 11 children. In a one block area there could be 60 children," Yvonne said, reliving those early years when, as a single parent of four, she welcomed many of those neighbourhood youngsters into her own home. "The kids all played in the street and in the back lane. They played hockey in the street and yelled out 'car' when a car came by." It was a safe place where people looked out for each other: a place where kids could really be kids. The Prior children always had something to do, someone to hang out with, and with Grandma now living with them, Yvonne had the comfort of extended family always nearby.

The Point was also a place where children were important—so much so that in 1948, after recognizing the need for the many boys living in the neighbourhood to have good, healthy activities to participate in, a young Leo Mell and his friend, Jules Barriere, started up a softball team. It went on to prove the adage, "from small beginnings come great things." In its founding year, the fledgling team took the City of Montréal Softball Championship and repeated the feat in 1949. By 1950, Mell and Barriere decided to expand into two teams in order to accommodate more of the area's youth.

But a year later, tragedy struck. Leo died of leukemia. He was only 20 years old. His friends and family, though heartbroken at their loss, put aside their grief and continued to build on Leo's dreams. Leo's brother, Joe, joined forces with Barriere and others. More teams were formed; girls' teams were added. Former Point resident David O'Neill explained, "what happened from this small activity was that the organization grew from one team to more than 110 teams, representing all major sports activities within the community." These teams took the name "Leo's Boys," in honour of their founder. Eventually team jackets were designed.

A few years later, the Pointe Saint-Charles Boys and Girls Club was also formed. Neighbourhood kids of all ages now had a building where they could gather to play games or sports, like ping-pong or basketball, or just hang out, and because the club shared a common interest in working with youth, many of its workers were also involved with the Leo's Boys, and Leo's Boys events were sometimes hosted there. ∽

EVERYDAY JOYS

Because the Boys and Girls Club was a few short blocks from the Prior home, Sharron became a member of the club at the tender age of six. It's where she spent many hours playing team sports with her friends. It's also where she honed her love for all things artistic and, when she turned 13 and became part of the teen centre, it's where she learned to do the Harlem Shuffle—the traditional step dance everyone in the area did to the 1963 hit single of the same name, also known as "The Pointe Saint-Charles National Anthem."

Hardly a day passed that Sharron didn't stop by the club for one reason or another, and on March 29, 1975, the 16-year-old was heading there to get her Leo's Boys jacket. To earn the bomber-style jacket with white leather sleeves, kelly green body and a Leo's Boys crest on the front left and across the back, Sharron had to sell a few books of raffle tickets. "We in the community had never before seen jackets of that type and quality," O'Neill said. "It was for us, as children growing up, something to die for…and that something to die for also generated pride in its wearing when one associated with other communities."

Like all her friends, Sharron was anxious to cash in her ticket money and take home her prize. At 3:45 PM that fateful Easter Saturday, she left her home on Congregation Street and, with her four-year-old foster brother Steven by her side, made her way down to the Boys and Girls Club to cash in her tickets and pick up her jacket. It turned out they didn't have her size, so she was given a receipt to pick up her jacket later, though she was thinking about passing on a jacket for herself and ordering one for Steven, who was in need of a spring coat. In the meantime, her girlfriend's jacket had come in, so Sharron agreed to deliver it to her on her way home.

Easter is traditionally a time of rebirth and regeneration: a time of promise. It's no accident that the Christian celebration of Christ's resurrection is held at the time of year when birds are once again chirping, buds are forming on tree branches and the world is generally emerging from the hibernation that comes with winter. Kids were outside playing that Saturday as Sharron and Steven meandered their way back to Congregation Street. Skipping ropes were twirling, bolo-bats bopping, moms were out pushing prams and everything generally felt well with the world.

At the Prior residence, Yvonne was busy getting ready for the family's big Easter dinner that weekend and preparing a pot of stew for supper later that day. Before Sharron had left for the Boys and Girls Club, she'd boiled eight eggs, set them in eggcups to cool and then painted the exposed half of each egg. When she got back from her errand, the eggs were dry, ready to be flipped and painted on the other side. While she was decorating the Easter eggs, Reverend Charles Cochrane, a family friend and the minister in charge of Melville Presbyterian Church in nearby Westmount, came by to give the family his best wishes. By the time he left, Sharron's eggs were painted, and Grandma, Mom and all five children sat down to a supper of stew and biscuits.

After dinner, as Sharron and her sisters helped clear the table, one of Sharron's friends stopped by for a visit. The girls chatted while Sharron readied herself for a night out with her friends, trying on one outfit after another before finally deciding to wear one of her mother's tops.

"She was at the table brushing her hair when I asked her what she was up to that night," Yvonne remembered. "I asked her if she was going to see her boyfriend, John, and she said she might, but had no confirmed plans about that one way or the other."

Sharron and her friends often met up at Marina's Pizzeria, a local hangout where the neighbourhood kids congregated. They would grab a pop and talk about their day, the latest styles, boys or whatever else was on their minds. And that's really all she was planning to do that night. The pizza place was a few short blocks from the Prior home, and at 7:10 PM Sharron shouted her goodbyes to her mom and bounced down the stairs a few steps behind her friend, who by then had crossed the street and was talking to friends. The last words Yvonne said to her daughter were "Goodbye" and "Be careful." It was a mantra Yvonne echoed behind her vivacious and outgoing Sharron every time she left the house.

The Point might have been a family-friendly neighbourhood, but it wasn't far from Chateauguay, an off-island suburb of Montréal located on the South Shore. The previous July, the body of 12-year-old Norma O'Brien had been discovered almost a half kilometre from her family's Chateauguay home. She'd been raped and murdered, and a hairbrush had been stuck in her throat. The story was never far from Yvonne's mind when any of her girls left the house. But she trusted Sharron, knew she had a good head on her shoulders and a sensibility beyond her years. Sharron was reliable and punctual, and if ever there were a reason for her to miss her curfew, she'd call home.

On the night in question, Sharron didn't make curfew. And she didn't phone home. ❧

A NIGHTMARE BEGINS

"Around 1:00 AM I called her girlfriends, and they said they hadn't seen her and thought perhaps she might have met up with her boyfriend to go to a hockey game," Yvonne said. "Then I called her boyfriend's home, and his mother said he was not in but would get him to call me when he came home. About 15 minutes later he called and said he hadn't seen Sharron that night either—he'd been out playing cards with some friends."

By now, Yvonne was getting frantic with worry, and it got worse when a few minutes later one of Sharron's friends called back with some disturbing information. "She said, 'Mrs. Prior, I don't want to upset you but did you know that around 7:00 PM a woman was attacked near the pizzeria?'"

What Yvonne was about to learn cemented any fears she had for her daughter's safety and set the stage for a lifetime of unanswered questions.

It was getting dark, but that didn't worry 23-year-old Cheryl Roy. The friendly streets of Pointe St. Charles were safe, and a quick jaunt along Charon Street to Lebere Street and down Ash Avenue towards Wellington Street to the local pharmacy to buy diapers for her baby didn't seem at all a risky thing to do. Cheryl noticed a fellow with a squared-off moustache and his hands in his pockets pass by her. Intent on her mission, Cheryl didn't give the man much thought. But when she got to the corner of Wellington Street and Ash Avenue, she heard the rush of footsteps, and before she could turn around to see what all the

STOLEN INNOCENCE—SHARRON PRIOR

commotion was about, the man grabbed her around the waist with one arm and held a knife to her throat with the other. She fought the man as he tried to drag her to a laneway and, in a quiet and disturbingly calm manner, he told her she was a dead woman.

Cheryl wasn't giving up the fight, but she was terrified and growing weary, and just when she thought she couldn't battle her assailant any longer, a young girl and a boy who saw that a woman was in trouble rushed towards Cheryl and her attacker. The knife-wielding man ran off, and Cheryl dragged herself to a nearby house. News of the attack didn't get out into the local media until the next day. "You're not getting away from me. When I get through with you I'll cut you to pieces," Cheryl said, repeating the man's threats to a reporter from *The Montréal Star*.

Sharron's friends who were gathered at Marina's Pizzeria had noticed the commotion across the street and had seen the flash of police cars, and it wasn't long before others in the general vicinity were aware of the attack.

The news terrified Yvonne. Sharron had left the Prior home about 10 minutes after the attempted assault, and because Marina's Pizzeria was only half a block from the location where Cheryl Roy was initially grabbed, it wasn't unreasonable to worry that Sharron might have rushed right into the attacker.

The next few hours were agonizing for Yvonne, the promise of spring shattered by the dark night of Hades. "Everyone was searching. People were knocking down fences, going into empty lots, there was lots of noise—it was almost like a riot," she said, her voice getting more animated as she described the scene.

Years later, Reverend Cochrane wrote of that night and the next two days in his memoirs: "I spent Sunday afternoon and all Easter Monday, with nearly 200 others, searching every conceivable area for Sharron—backyards, laneways, abandoned buildings, and along the canal. We had no success; and the police were not much help."

Usually, a person has to be missing for 24 hours before the police are willing to get involved, and when they do, they usually start by ruling out the obvious possibilities. Yvonne first called the police about 2:00 AM that Easter Sunday. "The police answered my call and came to the house," Yvonne said, adding that they suggested she shouldn't worry too much—maybe she was away at a party and forgot to phone home. "But I said, 'Listen. There was an attack on a woman in the same direction where my daughter was going.' And the policeman just said to call him in the morning." ∽

POLICE GET INVOLVED

The next day, when Sharron still hadn't come home, Yvonne called the police again. This time they came to the Prior home and spoke with Yvonne in person, obtained a photo of her daughter and asked for details. Did Sharron seem upset, have itchy feet or appear dissatisfied? Would she have run away? These were the horrible questions every worried parent of a missing teen has to endure before an investigation heats up and branches out to other possibilities. It was a line of questioning that didn't last long, though. Yvonne was quick to explain that her daughter was a good girl, called home regularly and was always trustworthy. If the police thought Yvonne's description of Sharron was just the words of a loving mother, and not as objective as an investigator would like, they soon learned that Yvonne was proud, yes, but she was also accurate in her assessment of her daughter.

Everyone the police spoke with pretty much described Sharron the same way—happy, outgoing, reliable, dependable, kind and friendly were some of the adjectives used by those who knew her. Reverend Cochrane said Sharron was "a very superior youngster—popular, extremely pretty, well-mannered, and highly intelligent" and stressed that not coming home at night "was so out of character for the girl that there was cause for concern." Moreover, the logistics didn't jive. Sharron hadn't taken a purse when she left for the pizzeria, and her bus pass and any money she had was left in her room. If she had planned to run away, she'd have certainly made sure she had a few dollars in her pocket and at least some of her personal items.

By now, Yvonne was inconsolable. There was no doubt in her mind that something terrible had happened to her daughter. She could feel it in the pit of her stomach. A mother has a feeling about these things. And for Yvonne, what made matters worse was that the police didn't actually start looking for Sharron until Easter Monday. Her baby was out there, needing help, and the authorities had yet to organize an official search.

The next few days passed in one slow, torturous moment after another, with no foreseeable relief in sight. And then on Wednesday morning, Yvonne noticed a man she knew looking obviously upset and banging on a neighbour's door with a newspaper tucked under his arm. She called out the window to him. "I knew there was something bad in the newspaper," Yvonne said, explaining that she asked the man several times why he was so upset then asked him to show her the newspaper. "And he kept saying, 'Yvonne, don't look…don't look.'"

There, in the pages of the *Montréal-Matin*, and in almost every other local media outlet that day, Yvonne's worst fears were confirmed. At about 9:00 PM, Tuesday, April 1, the body of a young woman had been discovered in a patch of land owned by a Longueuil-area beekeeper, just a 30-minute drive from Pointe St. Charles. At first glance, the description of the girl fit Sharron's, but Yvonne wasn't sure if the girl in question was indeed her daughter, and police needed to be absolutely certain. She'd have to identify the body.

"The police asked me if there were any identification marks on Sharron's body, and I told them she had a mole at the hairline at the back of her neck. And when she was a baby and had a vaccination, she moved and instead of a vaccination circle she had a line." That's all the information police needed to confirm that the body they'd discovered was indeed that of the missing Pointe St. Charles girl.

Finding out your daughter is dead is tragic enough, but nothing could have prepared Yvonne and the Prior family for the gruesome details. Sharron had been raped and her petite 5-foot 3-inch body brutally beaten. An autopsy confirmed she'd received "multiple skull fractures." Detective Sergeant Jacques Dutrisac told reporters from *The Montréal Star* that Sharron was likely "still alive when they [the perpetrator or perpetrators] dumped her under the trees." In fact, she might have been alive up to 20 hours before her discovery, meaning that her horrible nightmare might have lasted for three full days. ❧

DISTURBING IMAGE

Sharron was found wearing the suede jacket she'd left home with on Saturday night, the one she was worried about ruining in the light rain that began falling before she started out for the pizzeria. She was also wearing her sweater, socks and a pair of brown-lace, wedge-heeled shoes she'd borrowed from a friend. In her cold, small fist she clenched a cluster of branches. Bits of tape were caught in her knotted hair. Her panties hung on a nearby tree, and her jeans were found dumped a few feet away from her body. It would be a few days before the public heard about how Sharron's beautiful face had been battered and bruised, her jaw fractured, her nose broken and a hole torn through her cheek. The autopsy results stated that Sharron died from "asphyxiation caused by blood in her lungs."

Among the most telling evidence at the scene was a footprint, shoe size 8½, that was significantly indented to suggest the person who made it was on the heavier side, weighing about 200 pounds. No other footprints were discovered, and police surmised that the same person who had opened the gate lock to the small parcel of land where Sharon's body was discovered had made the single print. A man's shirt, with a 17-inch collar and 34-inch sleeves, was also found at the scene, and investigators theorized that the shirt may have been used as a restraint. Police weren't sure if the shirt belonged to Sharron or to the person involved in the attack. Although no draglines from tire marks were left behind the vehicle that was used to transport Sharron's body to the location, indicating she had been dragged, there was a blood trail. That blood trail meant she could have been carried to the site, but it was more likely that she had been thrown from a vehicle.

Perhaps the most significant discovery was the area where Sharron's body was discovered. The beekeeper's field, as it was referred to in news stories, was located at Chemin du Lac and Guimond Boulevard and had seen multiple abuses in its day. Passersby frequently used the spot as a dumping ground, so "the beekeeper," as Jacques Bertrand came to be known in the media, decided to deal with the problem by installing a gate, lock and all. It was Bertrand who discovered Sharron's body after receiving a telephone call from a friend. On Tuesday morning, this friend told Bertrand that his gate was open, so later that day, in among all his other chores, he checked it out, and what he found changed his life forever. "It really affected him," Bertrand's wife told Michelle McNamara of *True Crime Diary*. According to news reports, only two people had the key to that lock. But when Sharron was discovered, the gate's padlock was found unlocked.

"He [Bertrand] was under a lot of pressure because they [Bertrand and an unnamed partner] had the only two keys to the lock," Yvonne said. At one point in the investigation, an officer was quoted by the media as saying, "If we find the guy who opened the padlock, I think we will find the guy who did this." Horrifying words for Bertrand and his partner, who had to face the unpleasantness of being questioned. Both men were immediately cleared of any suspicion, but now that the key holders were quickly ruled out as possible suspects in the murder case, investigators had to look at other scenarios to explain the unlocked gate. Had the gate been properly locked in the first place? If Bertrand's memory was accurate, there was no doubt the gate was locked tight. Although it's highly unlikely, it is possible to pick some locks, and investigators had to examine the lock to see whether it had been forced open. Negative. There were no signs that the lock had been tampered with.

Police then had to explore the possibility that one of the two accounted-for keys had been duplicated without Bertrand or his partner knowing. Another possible scenario suggested that whoever dumped Sharron's body was likely familiar with the area and believed her body wouldn't be discovered until bee-keeping season commenced later that spring. The perpetrator could have taken down the stamping information on the back of the lock and deciphered the key code. That would have enabled him to duplicate the key without the original. Some might argue that one of these scenarios could point to a premeditated crime—to a planned murder. Was this a possibility? ∾

ON THE HUNT

Now that Sharron's body had been discovered, the investigation into her abduction, rape and murder was going full bore. As many as 38 individuals were questioned, including a man who folks at The Point referred to as the "motorcycle guy"—a man who belonged to a motorcycle gang and was suspected, but never convicted, of attacking Cheryl Roy. About four of those 38 were considered persons of interest. Sadly, for the Prior family and everyone involved in the case, none of those leads panned out with anything concrete.

The news of Sharron's brutal slaying made headlines for a few weeks, and then media interest in the story petered out. In 1976, a year after Sharron's rape and murder, the case was revisited with the hope of keeping it in the public eye, but the police couldn't really add much to the story. And although investigators continued to work on solving the murder, new crimes continued to increase their workload and diminished the amount of time they could dedicate to the Prior case.

A few other murders had occurred in the area, some of which remain unsolved, and in an otherwise quiet and family-friendly neighbourhood, it was clear that crime and its repercussions were seeping into the area. In January 1976, a 10-year-old newspaper carrier was found murdered in a back lane in Ville St-Laurent. He had attended the same Sunday school as Sharron had years earlier. Police questioned Yvonne and her daughters after someone at the boy's funeral mentioned Sharron's unsolved case and the possibility of there being a connection between the two, but nothing developed out of the thread. A little while later, Yvonne heard rumours about a third murder, this time a girl a little older than Sharron. Again, no firm connection between the cases was made.

On March 12, 1981, 12-year-old Tammy Leaky was abducted in the same vicinity as Sharron had been in 1975. Tammy was visiting her grandmother in The Point when she disappeared. She, too, was discovered raped and murdered and dumped a good 25-minute drive from Pointe St. Charles. As with the others, Tammy Leaky's murder was soon another cold-case file and remains that way to this day. ∾

A CHANGE OF FORTUNE?

In 2002, Yvonne finally got some good news. The police were starting the preliminary work required to re-open Sharron's case, and in 2004, her rape and murder was once again a focal point for investigators.

"When they re-opened the case, there were two detectives and they were really wonderful. They worked two or three solid years on it," Yvonne said. "One of them told me they had Sharron's picture right on the website. He said, 'That's my main picture, to remind me what I'm working on.'"

One of the first things the investigators did was conduct a DNA test on the man suspected of attacking Cheryl Roy. Apparently the suspect, who had a history of criminal activities, had been murdered, and his DNA was on file with the police. It was an easy check. When the results came in, the officers were surprised to learn there was no match. The suspect in the Roy case wasn't the man responsible for Sharron's murder. Ruling him out, on the other hand, wasn't entirely negative. Knowing their main suspect was 99-percent cleared meant police could look more closely at other leads.

One pressing tip that caused considerable furor in 2004 surrounded the theory that Sharron could have been held captive in a garage behind an apartment on Favard Street, not far from the Prior home. Although the Priors weren't overly familiar with the family who lived there in 1975, they were acquainted with them. On Wednesday, July29, 2004, police officers and a team of forensics descended on the garage in question, searching the walls and floors for blood trace evidence. At the time, investigators were hoping to find DNA evidence that might have propelled the investigation forward. Sadly, nothing conclusive came of the search.

As the years passed, the Prior family continued to mourn, and they remained vigilant in their quest to find Sharron's killer. In 2005, Yvonne and her twin daughters, Doreen and Moreen, met with the beekeeper and his wife for the first time. It was 30 years after Sharron's brutal murder, but the family wanted to hear the story of Sharron's discovery from the man who, until then, was little more than an abstract image in their minds. They wanted to hear the details again, this time from a new voice. Maybe Bertrand's rendition would spark new ideas, and with his help, the Prior women might come up with an untried theory. Bertrand was gracious and forthcoming. He even agreed to take the Prior women to the field he once owned.

"We were very excited that at last we found him...but at the same time apprehensive," Yvonne said.

Yvonne, her daughters, and a family friend who'd agreed to drive the Priors, met Bertrand and his wife for a cup of coffee.

"We met in his area in Longueuil...he was a very nice and gentle man.... We sat there for about an hour and a half or so...I was listening to it all but not really there. The whole thing was a little bit too much for me.

"I do remember saying to him, when everyone was ready to leave, I just wanted to see [where Sharron was discovered]. I asked him if he could take me there, and he said, 'why certainly, if [you] would like.'" Yvonne's voice softens as she relives the memory. Yvonne was 37 when her daughter died. She's 71 now. The pain she felt that day in the field, and the pain she still feels today, is as fresh as it was the day she discovered her daughter's fate.

"I was just looking—it's a vacant lot now. Doreen and Moreen were asking questions. I didn't remember being there before, but later I remembered that about five years after the murder I asked my friend to take me there, but I couldn't get out of the car.

"It was like a thicket—they [news stories] kept calling it a field but it wasn't a field. I would call it a little notch in the woods. A little alcove. Just big enough for [Bertrand's] beehives. It was surrounded by trees. If a car or truck drove in, the driver would not be able to make a turn in that small area. He would have to back up to get out."

Yvonne struggles with her words and pauses for a moment before going on. "This is what I wrote that day, 'Just a small alcove cut out in the woods. I felt numb. And could see photos in my mind of what took place there 30 years ago. My daughter lay dying. Alone. With no one to hold her hand.'"

That a young girl is brutally raped and murdered is beyond comprehension to most of us. It's the thing of movies, not real life. It should never happen.

That a murderer goes unnamed, unapprehended and unpunished is beyond belief. ∾

STILL ON THE BOOKS

The police continue to check up on leads from time to time. It's hard to imagine that someone who committed such a vicious and cruel brutality on another human being would have stopped at one murder. One has to question if he simply moved around, avoiding detection, or maybe he was in jail. Maybe he was even dead. Regardless of this predator's whereabouts, Yvonne and her daughters are relentless in their quest to name him. Discovering why someone would have robbed the world of this adorable young woman whom her family calls their "angel" is a question that might never be answered. But even if the man is dead, the Prior family still needs an answer to the "who" question. It's the final step down a long and pitted road to closing this drawn-out chapter of their lives. It's the final journey to healing—for everyone involved.

The Prior family has established a website in Sharron's memory. Along with news clippings on the murder, a brief outline about her and several stories on the scholarship fund established in Sharron's memory, there is a guestbook. More than

150 messages have been written in this cyberspace album as of the printing of this book. Most are from friends and family, sharing a special memory about Sharron. Some come from folks offering a possible tip or a new insight into the case. Thirty-four years after the murder, these messages are a collective testament to the huge affect Sharron's death had on so many people. Sharron was the girl next door. She represents any one of us who could have been walking down the lane that day, never to see our family again.

The Priors will not rest, even in death, until the person who robbed the world of this beautiful and talented young woman, so ready to give all she had and who dreamed of some day becoming a veterinarian, is caught. There are many generations of Prior children to come. Be sure that, in time, Sharron Prior's murderer will be named.

Chapter Three

Missed Opportunities— Theresa Allore

Autumn descends vividly on the Eastern Townships of Québec. A carpet of red, orange and gold blankets the landscape, the slight bite in the air whispers of winter, and squirrels are busily hoarding goodies for the leaner months ahead.

By early November it's usually crisp enough outside to warrant a few layers of clothing, but in 1978, folks in Lennoxville were still enjoying unseasonably warm temperatures. So much so that on Friday, November 3, Theresa Allore skipped her socks when she threw on a pair of Chinese slippers and chose a beige sweater-coat to wear outside instead of a fall jacket. She wrapped a favourite green scarf around her neck—a gift from her mother on her 19th birthday—and headed out for the last day of classes before the weekend. Rushing down the stairs from her dormitory room on the second floor of Gillard House, Theresa then bolted across the lawn for breakfast at the neighbouring

King's Hall dining room, talked about weekend plans with girl-friends Jo-Anne Laurie and Caroline Greenwood and then headed out to catch the bus to the main campus of Champlain College.

Caroline had invited Theresa to her family's farm for the weekend, but Theresa took a rain check on the offer. She'd intended to devote the majority of her weekend to a book report she was writing on Zen Buddhism. It was an important component of her psychology class, and Theresa was a determined student who spent the time required to maintain her high marks.

The day passed as it did on any other school day, and Theresa later met up with another friend during supper, this time at the dining hall at Champlain College. The two girls talked, and Theresa borrowed a cigarette, telling her friend that she was going to the library to work on a report. After agreeing to spin a few tunes later that evening at their Gillard House dorm, the two parted company.

Theresa never showed up to listen to music that night. But her absence didn't really raise any alarm bells. Theresa was a free-spirited young woman, and her plans could have changed unexpectedly.

The next couple of days whizzed by, as college weekends tend to do. Some of Theresa's friends recalled banging on her door when they returned from their weekend excursions, anxious to share what they'd been up to, but they couldn't find Theresa. Worried though they may have been, no one felt comfortable enough to raise the alarm: Theresa didn't like to be fussed over and often warned her friends not to treat her like they were "her parents." Days passed. Teachers didn't appear worried; according to some reports, the college faculty hadn't even noticed her absence. Finally, on November 10, a full week after Theresa was last seen, her 18-year-old brother, Andre, also a student at the college and a resident of King's Hall, took action. ❧

CAMPUS LIFE

Québec's Champlain College isn't like many other post-secondary institutions in other parts of the country. Generally speaking, students in the primarily French-speaking province graduate at the grade 11 level, but if they want to continue on to university, they must attend a CEGEP—a "College d'enseignment general et professionnel," or "College of General and Vocational Education." There, they obtain the equivalent of tailored grade 12 and 13, giving them a solid foundation for the direction of their future studies and, basically, the first year of their university program.

Champlain College is one of five English-speaking CEGEPs in Québec and is located on the stately, historic Bishop's University campus, which was established by an Act of Parliament in 1843. The CEGEP was founded more than a century later, in 1971, and from its inception the two institutions shared some of their facilities, including dormitories. Of course that couldn't last for long. With a steadily growing student population,

Champlain required its own residence. Today, the Champlain Regional College Residence Complex, sporting fully furnished apartments, provides students with all the comforts of home and is just a short walk from the campus. The residence's proximity to school, along with having onsite staff and clearly laid-out rules dictating regulations for students living in residence, as well as an overall "Code for Student Conduct, Lennoxville Campus," gives students and their parents a sense of security.

In 2002, the City of Sherbrooke annexed Lennoxville, which made it a borough of the much larger city, a privilege that also brought with it many amenities. But in the 1970s, both the community and the college facilities were different. Lennoxville was a small, independent community of a few thousand people. Because it was also home to several other schools, during the academic year, the town's population traditionally doubled in size. As early as 1978, the number of young people attending Champlain had grown to such an extent that it was clear they couldn't wait any longer to turn the sod on a new residence to provide housing for all the students who needed a place to call home for the school year. In the interim, the college had to make alternative arrangements for its students.

Eight miles away, in the rural village of Compton, stood an old Victorian-style mansion that was once used as a girl's boarding school. Proudly situated beside the aptly named King's Hall was the large, brick Gillard House, and college administrators believed the two buildings would work nicely as dormitory and dining hall for their students until a new residence was built at the campus site. There were problems, however. Reliable transportation between the campus and residence was an issue. Shuttle bus scheduling sometimes left a lot to be desired: the bus often left the campus before the end of classes and, during the evening, if you missed the 6:15 PM shuttle, you were out of luck until the next one made its rounds at 11:00 PM.

Some would later suggest that the Compton residence was also deficient when it came to supervisory policies. Given that more than half the students living there were under the age of 18, King's Hall and Gillard House were surprisingly lax when it came to such things as monitoring the well-being of the approximately 240 residents. Perhaps the problem was that all the bugs hadn't been ironed out when it came to routine supervision and the other safety measures for the makeshift dorm, but at the time, it was generally understood that room checks and curfews were pretty much non-existent, and students were encouraged to be as independent as possible.

According to several reports, including those in the student newspaper at the time and comments from students willing to speak about Theresa's disappearance, the site director was frequently absent from his post, and wild parties with students indulging in everything from beer and pot to LSD were so common that a night watchman, getting nowhere in sharing his concerns with college administrators, reportedly quit his job in frustration. A short while later, three other staff members resigned. King's Hall was shut down, and residents were reshuffled within Gillard Hall. ∾

A NEW SCHOOL YEAR

It was into this chaotic environment that Theresa Allore re-entered her studies after working for a year in a ski factory and sharing an apartment with friends in nearby Pointe Claire, Québec. That year away from the classroom gave her a clearer understanding of what she wanted to do with her education and career choices. She returned to the world of academe, focused on her studies and able to take care of herself.

But she was still an adventurous young woman who enjoyed her friends and took part in risky sports such as rock-climbing and skydiving. Authorities later suggested that Theresa's tendency to push the limits and take the occasional risk were some of the reasons why alarm bells didn't sound when her friends first noticed her missing, even after a week had passed since anyone could remember speaking to her. School officials reasoned that she probably took off on some wild adventure of her own making—if they pretended that nothing had happened, she would likely make her way home eventually.

Theresa's brother was the first person to officially comment on his sister's long absence. In 2005, Andre told CTV's W5 reporters that he first went to the college administration, asking them to look for his sister, only to be told that they "weren't about to turn the school upside down for a missing student." He then called his parents, who had moved with their youngest son, 14-year-old John, to St. John, New Brunswick, the previous summer. Andre explained the situation to his parents. Without a second thought, they loaded their car and began the long drive back to Québec, pausing only long enough to call in and report their daughter missing to the Lennoxville Police.

If the Allores were expecting a sympathetic and systematic investigation into their daughter's disappearance upon arriving in Québec, they were disappointed on both accounts. Mr. Allore combed the neighbourhoods in Lennoxville and Compton and all rural points in between, flashing his daughter's picture on front porches everywhere and hoping against hope that someone remembered something about his little girl. The way the Allores saw the situation, the police seemed to find it easier to label Theresa a runaway than to listen to the entire story or to question any of her friends or teachers. The adventurous young woman with a good head on her shoulders had suddenly, in the six weeks since classes began that fall, become an unpredictable vixen that loved to party and pop LSD, at least in the eyes of some of the authorities. It didn't matter how loudly Theresa's friends and family argued against the picture the police and some school officials had painted of her, the authorities maintained their tunnel vision.

In 2008, Theresa's brother, John, and investigative reporter Patricia Pearson co-authored the story, "What Happened to Theresa Allore." The piece, printed in the book *Criminal Investigative Failures*, by D. Kim Rossmo, includes a comment of Corporal Roch Gaudreault of the Sûreté du Québec (Québec's provincial police force headquartered in Montréal). Early on in the investigation, Gaudreault allegedly told Mr. Allore that "there was little they could do now, and that Theresa's body would probably turn up when the snow melted."

Lennoxville Police Chief Leo Hamel suggested that Theresa, perhaps motivated by her alleged involvement in the drug culture, may have bolted for the border, crossing over to Vermont. In the initial stages of the search for answers in Theresa's disappearance, Hamel sent a picture of the young woman to Vermont's border officers. And if these negative suggestions weren't coming from the police, they were coming from the school. In one instance, Dr. Bill Matson, the campus director at the time, painted such a bleak picture of Theresa that Mr. Allore wrote in his personal notes that it was suggested she had developed "lesbian tendencies," and that "if found, would need psychiatric treatment, by court order if necessary."

The Allores were devastated. These descriptions, these patterns of behaviour, didn't seem at all like the daughter they knew. They'd seen her a few weeks before her disappearance when she and Andre had returned home for Thanksgiving weekend. Nothing seemed amiss at that time. And if Theresa had started to display disturbing behaviours, surely Andre would have talked to his parents about it, especially after she went missing.

Everything in their hearts told the Allores that it was inconceivable their daughter could have changed so dramatically overnight. But there were all those rumours of wild parties. Alcohol. Marijuana. LSD. All these things were so foreign to the senior Allores that even though all the propaganda the authorities were spreading about Theresa went against everything they knew of her, they started resigning themselves to the possibility that her new environment may have corrupted her. At the same time, though, Theresa was their daughter, regardless what she may have gotten herself into. And they were going to do everything they could to discover what had happened to her; like any other missing person, Theresa deserved everybody's best efforts.

Ignoring the advice of Gaudreault and other officers, the Allores didn't just pack up, go home and wait for the snow to melt. They hired private detective Robert Beullac of the Bureau D'Investigation Metropol. It was Beullac, and not the local law enforcement, who went into overdrive, taking down statements from friends and faculty members who'd last seen Theresa. Beullac also noted important clues—such as Theresa's purse and hiking boots, both items she would have taken along with her had she any intention of being away for any length of time, were still in her room. ❧

POINTS LAST SEEN

Piecing together Theresa's movements on that fateful November 3 was Robert Beullac's first order of business. It was pretty clear how her day had started out: the clothing she wore, her breakfast at King's Hall, the declined invitation to visit her girlfriend's family's farm, and the bus ride she and her breakfast companions took to Champlain College were well documented. Because it appears taking roll call at the onset of any class was sporadic at best, it's not clear if Theresa attended all of her classes. But the friend who'd loaned Theresa a cigarette and made plans for the evening clearly remembered speaking to her around the supper hour. And it was quickly determined that Theresa had missed the 6:15 PM shuttle back to Compton.

Theresa's next move became the subject of much debate. Compton was about 12 kilometres away from the college. Did she start out walking and then try to thumb a ride home? Hitch-hiking was quite a common practice at the time. In fact, the student handbook provided tips on hitchhiking safely. Parents today might shudder at the thought, but back then it was certainly a feasible alternative and, likely in Theresa's mind, far more appealing than waiting at the campus for the next bus, scheduled to leave almost five hours later.

The problem was that no one ever came forward to say they'd given the missing girl a ride back to the residence, leaving police to develop the theory about why she never arrived home. It's part of what backed the theory that Theresa likely took off with that "lesbian lover" of hers or the "drug dealer" she'd supposedly become enamoured with.

On the other hand, Sharron Buzzee, one of Theresa's friends, swore up and down that she had bumped into Theresa on the steps of Gillard Hall around 9:00 on the night of November 3, which would have been about the time Theresa had planned to meet her other friend to listen to music. If Sharron's statement was true, that would mean Theresa had made it home safely, and that whatever had caused her disappearance happened some time after that 9:00 PM sighting. The problem was, police discounted Buzzee's statement. Indeed, if it was the only statement of its kind, one would be inclined to understand such a decision by law enforcement, but it wasn't.

Several other dormitory residents came forward to back Buzzee's claim, saying they too had seen Theresa that evening. But instead of acting on the practice of following all leads until they prove to be dead ends, the police simply tucked away the information in Theresa's file. Investigators stubbornly clung to their theory that the young woman was simply troubled and had allowed herself to get in with the wrong crowd; they didn't appear to actively pursue any other possibility.

Another factor reinforcing the theory backed by the Sûreté and Lennoxville police was that the Compton residence was known for its parties. On the night of Theresa's disappearance, in fact, there'd been a party involving LSD. Perhaps Theresa took part in the evening's festivities and had an adverse reaction to the drug? There's no telling how someone high on acid might react. But not one of Theresa's friends agreed with that scenario. All of them stated that although Theresa liked to party and smoked pot on occasion, she didn't take hard drugs. Even students who were at the party and had admitted to trying LSD that night said Theresa wasn't there.

It didn't matter. It appeared that the police had made up their minds. And Theresa's file turned colder than the coming winter.

That year, the turn of the seasons was more gloomy than usual for the Allore family. The large, Victorian home Theresa's parents had bought in New Brunswick was uncharacteristically solemn. Family gatherings were strained. And thoughts about what might have happened to Theresa were never far from anyone's mind. In John's story, he recalled sitting with his parents around the dinner table the Valentine's Day following Theresa's disappearance. The silent meal was disrupted by a piece of plaster falling from the ceiling. "It fell to the side of the table in the shape of a heart. I remember at that moment how I knew Theresa wasn't missing. She was dead." To the rest of the world, however, Theresa was still just a runaway. That all changed on one very black Good Friday. ∾

FROM MISSING TO DEAD

Friday, April 13, 1979, was Good Friday, a day of prayer and reflection for many of Québec's practising Christians. It was also a workday for many residents, including Robert Ride. The muskrat trapper was anxious to set his wire traps in preparation for that year's harvest. Making his way around the muddied shoreline of a pond located outside the village of Compton, Ride was probably securing a few baited float sets in three or four feet of water, or maybe nestling a few more stationary ones along the shoreline and not too far from a muskrat's nest. The work was time-consuming and painstaking; it was a circuit he'd repeat by wading along the shoreline to check on them two or three times throughout the day. If he was lucky, he'd snag himself a pretty good catch—between 25 and 50 muskrats would make it a really good day.

Intent on the task at hand, it took a while for Ride to notice something was amiss. Perhaps he was surveying the area, deciding which direction or plan of action to take. Maybe he was stretching or taking a few moments to regroup. Either way, something he saw in the distance struck him as out of the ordinary. At first he wondered why on earth someone would dump a mannequin in the woods—it's amazing the kind of mental leaps our mind makes to protect itself from life's cruel realities. No doubt his heart began to race as he inched his way closer and closer to the porcelain-looking object lying face down in about 8 to 10 inches of water and covered, slightly, by the tangle of shrubs and saplings and vines that lined the ground beneath the towering forest. As with such situations, reality merges into the unbelievable, and you can't help but wonder if you're dreaming. But this wasn't a dream.

In front of Robert lay the grey and decaying body of a young woman. She was wearing only her bra and panties. Her hair was matted. What was once a vibrant young life had been carelessly and unceremoniously discarded where, it was likely hoped, she would never be discovered—at least not for some time. The woman's body was found less than a kilometre from the village of Compton and the relative safety of Gillard House.

Corporal Roch Gaudreault of the Sûreté du Québec arrived at the scene a few minutes past 11:00 AM, an hour after Ride discovered a body that was soon determined to be that of Theresa Allore. The local coroner, Michel Durand, came on the scene shortly after that, along with a mobile crime unit. Soon, the otherwise quiet countryside, solemn with Good Friday mourning, mushroomed into a crime scene brimming with activity. Investigators combed the area, news photographers rallied to snap photos and to get as much as they could on the story for the next edition of their papers.

Bits and pieces of women's clothing were discovered that day. It was determined that most of it hadn't belonged to Theresa, but one treasured item did—the green scarf Theresa's mother had given her. It was torn in two, and the pieces were uncovered about 15 metres from each other. The watch Theresa wore that last day on campus was still on her left wrist, as were the ring she wore on her left forefinger and her earrings. Corporal Gaudreault noted what looked to be strangulation marks around Theresa's neck, and the information was included in the coroner's report.

By the next day, Theresa's body had been transported to the Chief Coroner's office in Montréal, and one of her former roommates, Joey Nice, was asked to try to make a positive identification. She couldn't positively identify Theresa, but she was pretty sure the clothing the investigators collected didn't belong to Theresa. By 11:30 that morning, Theresa's family had made it to the Laboratoire de médicine légale, preparing for a task no one should ever have to undertake. Theresa's father inched his way to the cold, metal table where it was quite likely the body of his only daughter lay, hoping against hope it wasn't her.

Through the tears that surely misted his eyes, Mr. Allore noticed a scar on the young woman's forehead and remembered the time he accidentally caught Theresa's forehead with the shovel he was using to clear the snow one winter. Still, a scar is hardly a positive identification. A dental analysis would have to do the job no one was able to complete. And so Mr. Allore had no other choice but to sign the paperwork required to perform yet another indignity to his daughter's body: her entire lower jaw would need to be removed to complete the analysis. While the Allores were coming to grips with the likelihood that their daughter's missing person's case had evolved into a murder and making plans for memorial services and funeral arrangements, the police continued with what Theresa's family and friends believed were surprising leaps of illogical thinking. Suddenly, this likely runaway was considered a possible suicide. Or perhaps she'd overdosed and, in a drug-induced hypnotic state, had wended her way into the woods surrounding Compton and removed her clothing before collapsing nearly naked in a pool of water, without anyone noticing even the slightest commotion. Or perhaps Theresa's death was the result of a drug trip gone bad, and panicked friends, worried about the trouble they'd get into for having allowed Theresa to become so incapacitated with illegal substances, had hauled her out of the Compton residences and into the woods and left her there to die, if by any chance she wasn't already dead.

If the Allores hoped their daughter's case would now get the attention it most assuredly deserved, they were about to be disappointed by investigators for a second time. Results from the dental examination confirmed the woman's body was indeed that of Theresa Allore. The coroner at the scene had already noted strangulation marks around Theresa's neck and bruises under her armpits. No traces of drugs and alcohol were in her system—with the body kept relatively intact over the winter, it was possible to make that determination. And yet still, suicide, drugs, even accidental drowning in the eight inches of water where she was discovered, seemed a more logical conclusion for the detectives working the case than murder.

The biggest question, of course, was why? ∾

PERCEPTION IS EVERYTHING

No one likes to admit defeat. In the extreme, the fear of failing is referred to, in medical terms, as atychiphobia. On the individual level, it can be paralyzing. It's no less damaging on the corporate level. If you were to take the story of Theresa Allore as an anomaly, you might, sadly, be able to overlook the behaviour of the police or, at worst, put it down to one poorly handled case. But on deeper examination of what was going on in the Eastern Townships at the time leading up to and surrounding Theresa's death, you might wonder if the reluctance of Québec's law enforcement to publicly speak out about any kind of criminal activities in the area had something to do with their concerns about public perception and perhaps an overarching fear of failure.

To hear the Lennoxville police tell it, the area was almost crime free. Sexual assaults against women and murder were the things of movies. Champlain's campus newspaper, *The Touchstone*, however, had a different view of life in that deceptively peaceful corner of the province. In January 1978, *The Touchstone* was just one of the student newspapers in the area to report three separate cases of assaults against women. The Lennoxville police downplayed these student news items.

While police chief Kasimir Kryslak was busy saying that in the "five years since he had been police chief there had been only one reported incident of sexual assault," student writers argued against the claim, saying that as many as eight rapes had occurred in the area in 1977 alone. In some of these stories, the perpetrator was described as being a short man wearing "jeans and a green parka." In other stories, the attacker is also short but has "black hair and a beard." The women attacked reported their experience to Champlain College and Bishop's University administration, as well as the police, but nothing was done. Even after Kryslak was replaced with Leo Hamel, nothing changed. It seemed as though the authorities believed these women were merely fabricating these stories. Theresa's disappearance, and then the discovery of her body, was just as easily ignored. John later said it was as if Theresa never existed. Indeed, it was like none of these women had ever existed and that none of their horrific experiences had occurred. ∾

HISTORY REVISITED

Theresa's death hit John hard. Not only was he beginning to wade through those awkward teen years when he lost his only sister, but he also grew up in a frustrating environment of secrecy, innuendo and shame. Despite Theresa's father keeping a journal with more than one year's worth of information he'd collected from college administrators, police, friends and a private detective, the senior Allores questioned how they might have failed their daughter. An emptiness had taken over the family when the vivacious redhead was lost to them. Understandably, a blanket of depression turned the usually happy household into a sombre one.

Eventually, frustrated with what he saw as Canada's way of hiding its dirt in file cabinets market "confidential," John decided to pick up and move south of the border. He fell in love with an American woman, married, welcomed three daughters into the world and settled into what in generous terms would be called a "fixer-upper" just outside Chapel Hill, North Carolina. John talks about the "Bad Dream House" in one of his online blogs, describing how the walls and ceilings, even the floors, were riddled with knife marks, how tin cans loaded with cigarette butts were scattered throughout the house and how only a bonfire would kill the overpowering smell of ammonia emanating from the urine-stained carpet. It was his wife who could see beyond the mayhem: "Trust me," she'd said.

A couple of months down the road, after John and his family had gutted and rebuilt the house and turned it into their home, they received an odd phone call from the police. They wanted to bring cadaver dogs onto their property and planned to empty and inspect their septic tank—just in case a woman's body had been dismembered and disposed of down the shaft. It turns out that the young man who had lived there with his widowed mother prior to the Allores purchasing the property was a major suspect in a murder investigation. The North Carolina police thought that the body of Deborah Key, who was reported missing on December 1, 1997, might be somewhere on the property that John and his wife purchased in 1999.

Deborah's body wasn't discovered, but the cadaver dog honed in on a scent in the crawl space underneath the house. The scent was so overpowering that the dog started pawing at the soil, shooting earth in every direction in a digging frenzy. Investigators joined in the effort as best as they could, but the space was cramped and difficult to get at. After hours of work, the officers came up empty handed. Reflecting on the experience, investigators theorized that Deborah was quite probably buried there at one time, and that the suspect had moved her body before the house could be checked.

The entire experience was unnerving to the Allores. As months passed, John witnessed the intensity with which investigators searched for evidence and fought for justice on behalf of Deborah Key. Sometimes John couldn't sleep at night. And he started to think back to Theresa's disappearance and the time when her body was found. He wondered why his sister's case hadn't drawn much attention. Why was it, in his view, simply brushed away? Even if one of the investigators' pet theories was correct, and his sister had succumbed to some kind of unfortunate accident, didn't Theresa's death deserve a conclusive answer? Didn't her family deserve to know what had happened to their loved one?

Theresa's father had already spent considerable time investigating the case in 1978 and 1979. Andre also returned to his sister's story, looking for answers more than a decade after her death. Now it was John's turn to dig. ∾

A Look at the Facts

In 2002, John Allore teamed up with Patricia Pearson, an old friend from his days as a youth in New Brunswick. Patricia was a former crime journalist, and in 1998, she had authored *When She Was Bad: Violent Women and The Myth of Innocence*, a book on women and crime that earned her the Arthur Ellis Award that year. Patricia knew where to dig and how to push the right buttons to get information. She also didn't buy the theory that frightened friends had dumped Theresa's naked body in the bush. It didn't make sense to her.

Patricia and John travelled to Québec's Eastern Townships, back to the halls of Champlain College, to the old police stations, to the grounds of King's Hall and Gillard House and to the streambed where Theresa's body was finally found. John writes:

> *The creek where she was found is about a mile outside the village, down what was then a gravel road into a valley and countryside farming fields. While driving there, it quickly became apparent that Theresa did not walk to this location. The spot is in the middle of nowhere. There is nothing around, just the empty foreboding of bare cornfields and overflowing creek beds made muddy from winter run off.*

Patricia and John stood in silence for a moment. They noticed a nearby driveway where, typically, farm implements would leave the main road and enter the field. Someone could have assaulted Theresa elsewhere and then transported her body to the location, parking on the access driveway while disposing of her body in the creek. "This was the place where I shed 20 years of vague, uninformed speculation and saw for the first time that my sister was murdered. Patricia echoed my thoughts… 'This was a sex crime,'" John wrote.

From the beginning, police publicly spoke out against the theory that Theresa had been murdered and possibly raped. One of the main reasons why police took this stand was because the coroner's autopsy was vague at best, simply stating Theresa had died a "violent death of undetermined nature." Any suggestion of signs of strangulation were omitted, but it was clearly determined that by the time her body was found, no bodily fluids could be recovered. Patricia contacted Dr. Kim Rossmo, shared what was known about Theresa's death and asked his opinion. With a PhD in criminology from Simon Fraser University, 21 years of experience as a veteran police officer, credited as the inventor of the investigative tool called geographic profiling and, as of this writing, holding the University Endowed Chair in Criminology and the Director of the Center for Geospatial Intelligence and Investigation (GII) in the Department of Criminal Justice at Texas State University, Rossmo's expertise provided another pair of eyes with an entirely different outlook.

On hearing the details surrounding Theresa's disappearance and death, Rossmo disagreed with the police assessment of the situation. Theresa could have indeed been a victim of rape. He explained that the absence of bodily fluids isn't uncommon in a decomposed body. And he posed another, interesting possibility: "The killer also might have used a condom. Or maybe he had a sexual dysfunction and couldn't engage in normal intercourse."

Then there was the matter of the toxicology report: Theresa was completely drug free. Neither illicit nor prescription drugs were found anywhere in her system—and because a person needs to be alive for drugs to work through their system, any trace of drug use would have been preserved in her vital organs through the winter months if she had died of an overdose. Instead of answers, John and Patricia were uncovering more and more questions.

After much prodding, Theresa's police file was handed over to John, albeit several pieces of information were removed in the interest of the Freedom of Information and Protection of Privacy Act. John couldn't see who the police questioned or the potential suspects they might have been considering. But he could compare the police reports to other sources, such as the coroner's report, and when he did, John noted a series of discrepancies and omissions. For example, the strangulation marks noticed by the coroner on the discovery of Theresa's body were recorded in his report but were absent from the police file.

Probing a little further, John asked Corporal Robert Theoret of the Sûreté du Québec, the officer who'd culled through Theresa's file before handing it over to John, if any DNA testing had been done to Theresa's panties and bra. John wasn't prepared for what he was about to hear next: his sister's underwear had been destroyed five years after her death. The logic behind that decision was as skewed as the rest of the investigation. "Limited storage capacity" and "we cannot keep things forever" were the reasons given for destroying the only material evidence of the entire case, which, at that point remained opened as an "unsolved crime."

By this time, John had discovered that, according to Gerald Cutting who was named Champlain College's head of student services in 1978, the Sûreté actually considered Theresa's death a murder as early as 1979. So why did they persist in telling Theresa's family otherwise? John pummelled Corporal Theoret with more questions: was anyone currently working on his sister's case; were any of Theresa's fellow students or teachers ever interviewed as suspects in the case; who were the main suspects? Theoret stood tight-lipped. Information on any of those questions wasn't forthcoming. ✐

NEW INFORMATION

John started rereading newspaper articles from the time of Theresa's death. Years earlier he had scoured over the English newspapers, but his French wasn't strong enough to grasp all the information in the French editions. Twenty-three years later that had changed, and his greater command of the French language opened up a library of previously undigested articles. It was through *La Tribune* that John learned of the discovery of 10-year-old Manon Dube's body near the village of Massawippi on March 24, 1978, also a Good Friday. A call to Robert Beullac, the detective hired by John's father in 1978, uncovered information about yet another dead woman. Twenty-year-old

Louise Camirand was found raped and savagely beaten to death near the village of Austin on March 25, 1977. The bodies of Dube and Camirand, as well as the body of Theresa, were all discovered between 16 and 32 kilometres south of Sherbrooke, and all three victims were last seen within a six-kilometre stretch in that same small city.

John was stunned by the new information he'd unearthed. Was it possible that his sister's death was in some way related to these other two cases? Could a serial killer have been operating in the area in the late 1970s? All three victims bore a striking similarity to one another when it came to their appearance, and although Manon was only 10, and some would argue a serial killer doesn't usually change his or her modus operandi and move from adult victims to children, at a cursory glance the young girl looked older than her age. Her autopsy led investigators to the conclusion that it wasn't likely she was sexually molested, which could have suggested an altogether different motive for her abduction and death.

One scenario posed by the police was that Manon was a victim of a hit and run, and the panicked driver had stopped to pick her up and dispose of her to try to avoid being caught. On the other hand, if her case was in any way connected to the others, the abductor might have noticed how young the girl was after her abduction and panicked, killed Manon by accident even, and then disposed of her body. In any event, at the very least, the stories of these young victims raised questions—far too many questions, some might argue, to be ignored.

In a report issued by Dr. Rossmo after he examined the three cases, as well as the geography of the abductions and subsequent body dumps, he suggested an argument in favour of looking at a serial killer could certainly be made. He suggested that the locations where the bodies were discovered formed a geographic pattern that to some degree coincided with each another. He also explained that serial killers typically live close to the area where they've met or abducted their victims and dump their bodies a safe distance from their homes. He states that, "three murders in a 19-month period, in such a tight geographic cluster, is highly suspicious. All were young, low-risk women. They were most probably attacked on the street, transported, and their bodies then dumped at a different location. The similarities are not likely the result of chance."

In an interview with *W5*, Rossmo points out that the rape and murder of Louise Camirand is proof that a sexual predator who wasn't afraid to kill was operating in the area at the time. Even if investigators didn't believe a significant thread tied the three women together, they should at least examine the possibility of a connection between them.

To be fair, the police involved in one or another of these suspected murders might not have been aware of the other cases. Until fairly recently, police districts often operated independently of one another. Over the years, it became clear that if police and law enforcement personnel across the country shared the details surrounding violent crimes, it could be beneficial in several ways. Sometimes criminals migrate from one area to another, committing crimes as they move along. Or they could have carried out their offences along convenient boundary lines between police jurisdictions. In both instances, officers investigating independently of one another wouldn't reap the advantage of having the full criminal profile, which significantly lowers their knowledge about an unidentified suspect and the possibility of apprehending a criminal.

In the 1970s, communication between different police jurisdictions wasn't as fluid as it is today. The advent of the information highway and investigative tools such as the Violent Crime Linkage Analysis System changed that. But it wasn't until January 2003—25 years after Theresa's murder and almost a decade after the system was considered a firmly established investigative tool in Canada—that her information was added. ∾

No New News

Not much has changed in the three decades since Theresa's death, as far as her case goes. Police are no closer to honing in on a key suspect or making an arrest. In June 2005, the Allore family received a small vindication when, in an official statement from the Québec government, it was formally acknowledged that the young woman was indeed a murder victim. Her death was not the result of an overdose. She didn't die accidentally. The statement acknowledged that because her clothing and other personal items had been scattered some distance from her body, it suggested some kind of struggle took place. And "given these facts, the Bureau de la révision administrative finds that Theresa Allore did not die a natural death and that the circumstances of her death were criminal in nature."

Although the police consider Theresa's death a cold case, the Allores believe it's anything but. John writes in an online blog, "Theresa's death has never been investigated as a murder. It's red hot; there are many leads to follow up on, at least three suspects that need to be rigorously pursued (before they die). I think after [three decades] of screw-ups, my family is owed—at least—full dedication to this matter."

For the innocent young woman whose life was stolen from her, nothing less is acceptable. For the families of Manon Dube and Louise Camirand, the same holds true. Their murders also remain on the books as unsolved crimes.

Chapter Four

Project Angel—Candace Derksen

Twenty-two years of wondering why. Twenty-two years of asking what kind of monster would squelch a flame so bright; who could so callously and brutally end a life so full of promise? With each passing day and with each sad anniversary, the people who remembered, those who still pondered the case and those who still missed the young girl with the bright, intense eyes and flamboyant personality, thought that a monster might walk. Maybe there would be no justice in this case, not in this lifetime anyway.

Then one day everything looked different. A sudden break in the case caused renewed public interest. An arrest had been made. And a family was catapulted back in time. ❧

NOVEMBER 1984

Winnipeg is notorious for its long and cold winters, but in 1984, it was as if the city was being given a reprieve for a time. By November, a carpet of snow and winter wear is usually the norm. Not that year. For the most part, the ground was still dry by the end of November, and what little snow that had fallen had quickly melted away. The temperature hovered around 20°C for the lion's share of the month, and most folks hadn't yet pulled their down-filled coats from the closet. I remember taking advantage of the nice weather, pushing a pram throughout our south-end neighbourhood, giving my new baby girl a chance to enjoy a little fresh air and trying to shed a few more pounds from my pregnancy before winter hit, as it surely would.

On that last day of November in 1984, 13-year-old Candace Derksen was also enjoying the nice weather. Dressed in jeans, a light polyester top, runners with shoelaces that were never tied and a light jacket, it was clear Candace wasn't worried about being cold. Snow that had fallen that afternoon hadn't melted away, and after school she found herself the recipient of one of the first face washes of the year. That September, having transferred to Mennonite Brethren Collegiate Institute (MBCI), a Christian school located near the foot of the Disraeli Bridge in the Elmwood area of Winnipeg, she'd just met 17-year-old David Wiebe, and the two were developing a fast friendship. It was David who gave Candace the face wash, and she was flattered by the attention.

She had a lot to be excited about that day. It was Friday, and Candace had planned a fun-filled Saturday and Sunday. Her best friend Heidi was coming to the Derksens for the weekend, and Candace could hardly wait. A few years earlier, the girls had met at Camp Arnes, an interdenominational Christian camp located about 112 kilometres north of the city on Lake Winnipeg. Because Heidi lived in the town of Arnes, and Candace lived in Winnipeg, the girls had to be content with a long-distance friendship dotted by occasional weekend visits. This was a sleepover a month in the making, and both girls were looking forward to it.

Perhaps it was Candace's excitement over her many planned activities that motivated Candace to call her mom for a ride home from school that day. The Derksens didn't live that far away from the school. Candace could have easily walked, and if she was in a hurry, the city bus would get her there faster than her feet would. Most times that's exactly what Candace did, but for some reason that day she phoned home.

Wilma, Candace's mother, was busy cleaning the basement family room and getting it ready for Heidi and Candace to take it over for the weekend when Candace called. Wilma still had a lot of work to do before she had to pick up her husband, Cliff, from work. With nine-year-old Odia and two-year-old Syras occupied by the television, Wilma had a little time to finish up the last of her chores. When Candace called, Wilma asked her if she would mind taking the bus. Wilma told Candace that if she managed to get her housework done quickly, she and Candace could go shopping later that night to pick out Candace's favourite party snacks for her sleepover. Candace told her mother it was no problem—she could walk. She also said she had money on her for bus fare. Either way, she'd be home soon. After a quick goodbye, Wilma returned to her housework, and Candace left the school.☙

SOMETHING'S NOT RIGHT

It wasn't long before Wilma noticed that haunting feeling most of us have experienced some time in our lives: it's an unsettled sensation in the pit of your stomach that sparks fear and worry for no other reason than you just know something's wrong. Wilma was second-guessing her decision to ask Candace to walk home. There was no reason Wilma should have worried. Theirs was a safe neighbourhood. Winnipeg was a safe city. But at that moment, in the midst of folding laundry and vacuuming, Wilma questioned herself. She could have left her chores and got back to them later that evening. Wilma often packed up the younger kids and drove over to the school when Candace called home for a ride. Now she was wishing she'd done the same thing that November day.

Wilma went upstairs, checked on her two youngsters enthralled with their television show and then looked outside. The fat snowflakes that started falling that afternoon no longer melted when they hit the ground. Now, a layer of white hid the browned grass underneath, and a noticeable bite in the air indicated a drop in temperature. She remembered Candace wasn't really dressed for cold weather. Worse still, it was almost time for Wilma to pick Cliff up from work, and Candace had yet to make it home. What was keeping her?

Switching off the television set, Wilma told Odia and Syras to get ready. They had to pile into the car to pick up Dad anyway, so Wilma decided to make a few rounds of the neighbourhood in the hope that she or Odia would spot Candace. By then it was rush hour, and everyone was in a hurry to get home and relax after a long workweek. Touring the back alleys meant Wilma could drive slowly and check thoroughly for Candace: it was harder to take her time along busy Talbot Avenue. She glanced into the windows of the 7-Eleven store as she drove by, thinking Candace might have stopped to pick up a treat. No luck. She drove to the school, just in case for some strange reason Candace hadn't left yet, but found the doors locked. By now, having to pick up Cliff from work was more than just another chore. "…I had this unreasonable sense of foreboding…I needed Cliff," Wilma wrote in her book, *Have You Seen Candace?*

Cliff was also concerned. It was so unlike Candace to be tardy, especially when she knew her actions would have an impact on the family's evening routine. Aside from shopping, Wilma and Cliff had to go to the bank, and Odia and Syras were looking forward to dinner at McDonald's. There was still so much to do in preparation for the family's weekend guest, and in her parents' estimation, Candace was far too thoughtful a girl to be late and not call home with a reason why.

The Derksens made their way back along Talbot Avenue again, this time with an extra pair of eyes scanning the streets and sidewalks now that Cliff had joined them. When they finally made it home, Wilma rushed into the house. She'd left the door unlocked in case Candace had arrived while she was away. Wilma hoped that's what happened: she hoped Candace's tardiness was nothing more than a teenager being distracted. But the house was empty. Candace wasn't at home.

Cliff decided to make another sweep of the path between the family's Herbert Avenue duplex and the school, and Wilma started calling Candace's friends. Wilma had asked both her daughters to write down the names and phone numbers of their friends, and this information was kept near the phone in case Wilma needed to get in touch with them on short notice. But it was quickly apparent that the list Candace had made up several months earlier wasn't current. Candace had a lot of new classmates now that she'd changed schools. Their names weren't on the list by the phone.

Wilma decided to call Candace's old friends first. If she didn't have any luck in locating her, she'd start phoning her daughter's new classmates. Candace kept her personal phone book in her bedroom, and Wilma had every confidence that because friends were so important to Candace, the phone book would be updated. As she made her way through the list of familiar names from Candace's elementary school, Wilma was encouraged by the response she was getting. Although these friends hadn't seen Candace, they agreed to call around, which meant even friends whose names weren't on the list would be contacted.

Wilma hadn't really had the opportunity to get to know many of Candace's new friends, but she found them as gracious and helpful as Candace's old friends when she called them. What she learned was that Candace had talked with a few of her friends, had hovered near the school phone around the time Wilma remembered her calling home and had battled in the snow with David before he had to leave for his driver's education class. Candace was last seen walking down Talbot Avenue, alone, and by all reports she was in a good mood.

By the time Wilma called every number she could find, it was around 7:30 PM. Cliff had returned home from his drive through the neighbourhood, with still no sign of Candace. The couple decided to do what any caring parent would likely do when faced with a similar situation—they called the police.

The Derksens might have thought the police would immediately rush out and start looking for their daughter, but that's not what happened. The majority of the time, in cases like this one, the police are reluctant to jump to the conclusion that something untoward might have happened. After all, it was only 7:30 PM; Candace had been missing just a few hours. All things being normal, chances were the young teen was with a friend somewhere and had lost track of time.

There was another possibility to consider. Something that would have never crossed the Derksens' mind but was one of the first things police thought about—Candace could be a runaway. According to the Missing Children Society of Canada, 60,582 children were reported missing in this country in 2007. The majority of those cases—46,189, or roughly 76 percent—were eventually discovered to be runaways. The numbers might be larger today than they were in 1984, but that most missing children leave home of their own free will was just as true in 1984 as it is today. And according to the police, who eventually met with Cliff and Wilma late that Friday night, there were "a hundred runaway teens on the streets of Winnipeg at any given time" and "any child over twelve who disappears [was] probably a runaway."

The Derksens couldn't believe what they were hearing. Candace had no reason to run away. There hadn't been any quarrel. She wasn't a rebellious daughter. She wasn't feeling overwhelmed by her family's religious background, as one police officer suggested. Theirs was a happy family. For the Derksens, the frightening possibility that their daughter was taken by force was far more likely—it was the only explanation they had for why Candace wasn't home right at that moment. Cliff and Wilma shared their concern that someone might be holding their daughter against her will. The police countered that worry by saying there hadn't been a stranger abduction in Winnipeg for almost a decade. What made the Derksens think this case was the result of such a rare occurrence? For the Derksens it was simple—there was no other reason for her absence. Nothing else made any sense. ∾

THE FIRST, LONG, DARK NIGHT

When the police left, the Derksens found they were struggling with an entirely new set of questions and worries. Could it be that they really didn't know their daughter? Was Candace, as the police suggested, just rebelling against her Christian upbringing? It was true that Candace had wanted to attend Elmwood High for grade seven. All her elementary school friends were going there. But Cliff and Wilma wanted their daughter to attend MBCI. Wilma had gone to a Christian school, and although there's never any guarantee that one environment is better than another, she had appreciated studying with a peer group that had parents with similar rules. She hadn't been the only one who couldn't wear makeup or smoke or dance: all her friends faced the same set of expectations from their parents. Wilma reasoned that because friends were so important to Candace, she wanted her daughter to surround herself with friends who were subject to the same rules. And even though attending the private school stretched the family budget to its limit, it was something Cliff and Wilma believed in so strongly that the resulting financial sacrifice wasn't even a deterrent.

Candace, however, could have changed all that. The Derksens made a deal with their daughter. They encouraged her to give MBCI a try. Just for one year, they suggested. If after the year she remained convinced that she wanted to attend Elmwood High, she could do so with her parents' blessing. Although it was only a few months into the new school year, the Derksens weren't worried that Candace would change her mind. By Friday of the first week of the new academic year, Candace was clearly thrilled with the school and was enjoying the new friends she was making. "You were right, Mom. They're my kind of people," Candace told her mom soon after starting at MBCI.

And Wilma detected no signs of dissatisfaction in Candace's voice during their telephone conversation on the Friday she went missing. Even David said Candace was in a good mood when he left her. Could everyone's perception be so far from reality? Was Candace really bitter and angry and a potential runaway as the police had suggested?

Wilma tried to make sense of it all, pacing the living room all night long and praying that the worst-case scenario was that Candace was indeed a runaway and was punishing her parents for some perceived frustration. The conversation with police sparked a few ideas for Cliff, and he decided to make some phone calls. He needed to know a little more about his daughter's state of mind earlier that day. If something was bothering her, he and Wilma needed to find out what that could have been.

One person Cliff telephoned suggested he call Dave Teigrob, MBCI's school counsellor. Candace had apparently seen him that day. Perhaps Teigrob would have an indication whether something was bothering their young teenager. It was nearing midnight, and Cliff's call woke Teigrob from what was likely a fitful sleep, but Teigrob didn't mind. He explained that his talk with Candace that Friday was routine. He said she seemed in good spirits and was pleased with her adjustment to MBCI; she had given him no sign she was distraught over anything.

Cliff shared the news with Wilma as the couple stood staring out their living room window and wondering where in this suddenly very large city their daughter could have disappeared? A few moments later, the ringing of the doorbell shook the quiet of the night. For a moment, the couple allowed themselves to hope. Perhaps their daughter was home! Instead, it was Teigrob standing there on the Derksens' front step. He couldn't sleep. Learning of Candace's disappearance was too unreal and too disturbing even for this teacher who had only started to get to know the young girl. The trio talked well into the night. It was 2:00 AM when the counsellor left for home, and the Derksens tried to get some sleep. Two young children had to wake up in the morning, and God only knew what their family would be dealing with the next day. Soon Cliff was sleeping; Wilma sensed he was still hopeful that Candace would come home. Wilma, on the other hand, was struggling with a deep, inner sense of foreboding.

She got up and wandered into her dark living room, stared out into the busy night and watched the vehicles driving on the Nairn overpass. Where was her Candace? Had she been hurt? Was she cold? Was she frightened? Wilma prayed. She drew on the hope that her faith provided. She asked God to bring her daughter home. And if that wasn't going to happen, Wilma prayed for God to wrap his loving arms around her darling Candace and protect her from any pain—"she couldn't bear pain," Wilma said. Wilma then noticed a sudden calm outside. It was like someone had turned off a switch. The wind, which had been howling since Wilma first started worrying about her daughter, suddenly stopped blowing. Was it a sign? Had Candace moved from this life to the next? ∾

GETTING MOBILE

Even before breakfast the next day, the first order of business that Saturday morning was to call Dave Loewen, Cliff's employer and the director of Camp Arnes. After listening to Cliff's version of the events of the night previous, Loewen suggested they form a volunteer search party. He said he'd make the necessary contacts with lawyers and police to ensure the group wouldn't hamper the police investigation. Shortly after that conversation, the two police officers from the evening before arrived at the Derksens. They were checking in and were clearly concerned about Candace's well-being, but they remained convinced that she'd run away.

The investigators asked to see Candace's room. Wilma welcomed the idea and showed the officers to her daughter's bedroom. They found the young girl's diary and started skimming through its contents, trying to get an understanding of Candace's state of mind. "See, she did have problems," one officer said. "This girl's in trouble."

Any parent of a young teen can tell you a youngster's private journal can be easily misinterpreted, especially when taken literally. Wilma acknowledged that Candace was like any other girl her age, going through the ups and downs of growing up, worrying about friends and school and thinking about boys. Young girls write about such things in their diaries. But there were other entries too; entries the police didn't appear to place the same emphasis on. Candace had written poetry in which she challenged herself to live a life that made a difference in the world, and there were heartfelt prayers she'd written to God. The police dismissed these entries.

A few hours later, after police started contacting Candace's friends and asking questions, they became more convinced than ever that the Derksens were the problem, that Cliff and Wilma had caused their daughter to bolt. One police officer even went so far as to elicit a commitment from Wilma that when her daughter came home, the family would go for counselling. Instead of arguing with the man, Wilma agreed. "I promise you…if you find her and bring her back to me, I'll go and see six psychiatrists if that's what you want me to do." She knew she wouldn't have to. By now, Wilma Derksen was pretty sure her daughter was dead.

But it was early days yet. Less than 24 hours had passed. It was critical that if there was even a remote hope that Candace was still alive and needing help, a search party would have to be mobilized soon. Loewen had called Dave DeFehr, Camp Arnes board president and prominent Winnipeg businessman, organized the logistics of the search based on police and legal advice and arranged a full force of about 30 searchers. By 1:00 PM these volunteers were ready to look for Candace.

The group divided into teams of two and three and was instructed to stay on public property unless owners gave them permission to go on their property. If anyone came across an abandoned building or shed that for some reason tweaked their interest, they couldn't enter without the owner being present. Any garbage placed at the side of the road was fair game. It could be opened and examined—once garbage is set on the curb it is considered public property.

The searchers started combing the neighbourhood between the Derksens' house and the school, but Wilma stayed home, torn between wanting to take part in the search and needing to be near the phone in case Candace or the police called with any news. Candace's friend, Heidi, and her dad stopped by—in all the stress of the previous night, Wilma had forgotten to call them and apprise them of the situation. They were shocked; Heidi broke down into tears.

At some point during the hustle and bustle of the day, David Wiebe's mother called and asked Wilma if the Derksens had any family nearby. Wilma explained to Mary Wiebe that their extended family lived in Saskatchewan and BC—Wilma's parents were called and were on their way but wouldn't arrive until Sunday to provide the young family with much-needed moral support. Concerned, Mary volunteered to come over to keep Wilma company. "No one should be alone at a time like this," she said. And even though Mary was a stranger to the Derksens, until the day before when Wilma had sought out David to ask him when he'd last seen Candace, Mary was quick to offer comfort and encouragement. Mary played with Syras, helped wherever she was a needed, listened to Wilma's story about Candace and kept saying, "Candace is in God's hands." Wilma later admitted she wasn't sure exactly what Mary meant by that comment, though it had been comforting to hear. Being reminded that God was there touched Wilma's heart and brought something akin to peace amid the chaos.

Although police were still insistent that Candace was likely just truant, the search team had started producing some unexpected results. The concern of the wider community and its self-motivated call to action was having an impact on law enforcement, as were the efforts of Harold Jantz, editor of *The Mennonite Brethren Herald*. Jantz was asked to tap into some of his media contacts to try to get a photograph of Candace into *The Winnipeg Sun*. It was just a matter of time before the rest of the media would be all over the story. Clearly, a lot of people were concerned about this missing girl and her family. Such support made it a whole lot harder for the public, and the police, to believe Candace was a troubled child with a difficult family life.

A wave of prayers was also being uttered throughout the city on Candace's behalf. The next day was Sunday. More people would know about the young girl's disappearance, and more people would be praying. The Derksens need not feel alone. As another day darkened and another long night loomed ahead, the Derksens tried to get some sleep. They knew they were being supported and upheld in so many ways, but any parent would struggle with feelings of helplessness, knowing that the child they had brought into the world with so much joy and hope for the future was out there, alone in the cold, and they could do nothing about it. The Derksens were no different. Sleep was a long time coming. ∾

SOLEMN SUNDAY

The sheer amount of energy and activity packed into a Saturday alone would exhaust most people for a week, but the journey into finding out what happened to their daughter was only beginning for the Derksens, and they had to soldier on. By the time church services were over that Sunday morning, the phone was ringing off the hook. Friends who'd just heard that Candace was missing wanted to share their concern. Visitors stopped by with food and offered more heartfelt prayers. There was no end to the offers of help—no request was too large.

As well, another search party was being organized. Reporters from *The Winnipeg Sun* and *The Winnipeg Free Press* had called, asking to hear about the Derksens' plight and preparing stories for the next day's issue of their respective papers. Soon the entire city would know that a young girl, excited about a fun weekend with her favourite girlfriend, never made it home after school two days earlier.

Most of us pride ourselves in being caring, loving people who are ready to lend a hand whenever it's required. Some of us thrive on volunteer service—it is really so much more rewarding to give than to receive. Folks are generally goodwilled; at least that's the way I choose to look at life. Perhaps that is why it was so hard for people to wrap their heads around Candace's story. I, too, remember sitting at home and reading those first news reports about Candace. Like many of my friends and family members at the time, I couldn't grasp the idea that something sinister could have happened to this young girl. So, like the police, I was far more comfortable thinking that Candace had run away. She'd had a fight with her mother and needed some time to cool off. That had to be the reason for her disappearance.

Stranger abductions just didn't happen in Winnipeg, especially in safe, small suburbs like Elmwood and the neighbouring East Kildonan area. Not long before Candace's disappearance, I, too, lived in that area, took the city bus late at night, walked those streets at all hours and didn't worry a bit about strange people lurking about and waiting to pounce on an unsuspecting pedestrian. But as I sat there, reading the newspaper and holding my new baby girl in my arms, I couldn't help but wonder…what if? What if the Derksens were right? What if a stranger had grabbed their daughter and was holding her against her will? I couldn't imagine what they must have been going through.

For weeks, the Derksens and their story took centre stage during most supper-hour newscasts. They also were guests of Peter Warren, an investigative reporter who, at the time, hosted a popular radio show on CJOB. Newspapers kept their reading public updated. And some of the publicity produced tips from good-hearted people who thought they had seen Candace or had seen something suspicious on Talbot Avenue on the day she went missing.

On the other hand, tragedy sometimes brings out the worst in people. Perhaps in not knowing all the facts, some people start to grasp at straws, make up stories and spread misinformation. Some of those hurtful rumours and innuendo, and the occasional case of mistaken identity, temporarily cast doubt on the picture Cliff and Wilma had painted of their good daughter. Whispers began to circulate that Candace was abused, that she was illegitimate—that she was not Cliff's daughter at all—that she was really a Native foster child, that she was living with friends and was "fine" and that the Derksens were separated.

Throughout it all, the Derksens held their heads high. In spite of the gossip, they clung to what they knew was the truth about their situation and trusted that they'd eventually get the answers they were looking for. But for the time being, when it came to concrete information, there wasn't much to share with the public. Despite several searches, more than 3000 flashy neon posters plastered around the city and the ongoing support of the police who, by that point, were starting to get a little more concerned themselves, there wasn't a single lead anyone could hold on to. It was as if the 13-year-old had simply vanished into thin air during one of the busiest times of the day on a busy city street. How can such a thing happen and no one remember seeing anything?

At some point in the investigation, the Derksens received an education on the criminal element from an unexpected source. Around 10:00 PM one evening, a stranger knocked on their door and offered his perspective on the possibilities surrounding Candace's disappearance. The stranger said he'd served nine years in jail. He knew something about life on the streets.

The fellow invited Cliff into his van. He said he'd take Cliff and his dad, who was visiting at the time, for a ride throughout the safe neighbourhood the Derksens believed they lived in and show them some of the seedy underbelly that's sadly part of many "safe" neighbourhoods. The man argued against Wilma's comment that Candace may have been picked up and transported out of the city by now. The stranger said that's generally not how criminals work, "they stay where they are; they don't travel around much."

As he drove, the man pointed out sheds and trailers and garages that should be searched. He explained how to "identify drug pushers' houses," and he pointed out where some of the city's Bravo motorcycle club members lived. When Cliff and his father finally returned home, Cliff shared what he'd learned with Wilma and his mother, who were waiting anxiously for the men's return. Would they ever feel safe again, they wondered? ◦◦

'TIS THE SEASON

Time stops for no one. In the midst of the Derksens' turmoil, Christmas carols still pealed out in shopping malls, offices and every other public place in the city, and coloured lights still flickered in living-room windows. Wilma's parents, who'd travelled from BC to be with their daughter and her family, had to return home. Christmas was coming. It wasn't so much the commercialization of the season that needed to be prepared for; it was the celebration of Christ's birth. The birth of that child 2000 years earlier gave the Derksens hope for the future. Somehow the grieving family would have to focus their energies on both their worry for their daughter and their faith that this world is at best temporary, and that the Prince of Peace had come to save us from all pain and suffering. Despite the chaos they were feeling, the Derksens believed that God was still in control. And there was also Odia and Syras to think about. Even though they missed their sister, the two youngsters needed a sense of normality.

The search continued, and the media maintained their interest in the case. Wilma and Cliff appeared in front of the camera again. Yet another search was being organized, along with prayer chains and prayer days. *It's A New Day*, a Christian television show hosted by Betty and Willard Thiessen, filmed a segment on the case. Although many Winnipeggers' hearts continued to ache for the Derksens, and the light of the Christmas season had considerably darkened for many residents because of this family's plight, others might have wondered why this particular young girl warranted such extensive attention.

According to Wilma's book, at that time in the city's history, there were 76 juveniles reported missing: 29 boys and 47 girls. Some of the parents of these youth were calling police, asking for similar efforts for their sons and daughters. Wilma and Cliff couldn't respond to the comments in any other way than to continue to focus all their energies on finding their daughter; they were getting a lot of help, but for worried parents it's never enough. Their hearts went out to other families with missing children, but they had to concentrate on their daughter—their nightmare.

When asked by the media how they thought they'd feel if Candace came home—if she would be embarrassed by all the attention—the Derksens dismissed the idea. Candace would have loved the attention, Wilma said. And if getting their daughter back meant they'd suffer public humiliation, they would gladly accept that. As the old year faded and a new one began, chances of experiencing a happy embarrassment appeared less and less likely, even to the few diehard believers who still thought that Candace was a runaway. ∽

One Answer, Many More Questions

Seven weeks into Candace's disappearance, Wilma, distracted from her household chores by thoughts of Candace and the investigation surrounding her disappearance, found herself staring out the window and noticing a neighbour "doing something that was uncharacteristic." When the man noticed Wilma watching him, he looked unsettled, and then he disappeared. The individual was someone Cliff and Wilma had wondered about earlier; he was someone Candace was appalled by. Wilma remembered the police saying that if Candace was indeed abducted, chances were it was by someone the family, and perhaps even Candace herself, knew. As Wilma explains in her account of this terrible time in their lives, the man was the only person in the Derksens' circle of acquaintances who didn't sit right with them. Wilma was suspicious.

The next day, still unable to get this neighbour out of her mind, Wilma confided her thoughts to Cliff. They decided to go to the authorities with their suspicions, something they'd done once before about this man, and after picking up Syras from the babysitters, the Derksens pulled up to the police station. It was Thursday, January 16, 1985.

They thought it strange how the chatter they heard upon entering the station silenced suddenly, like someone had punched the mute button on a television remote control. The Derksens felt self-conscious, wondering if they'd broken some unspoken rule by showing up there. They tried to talk to anyone who would listen to them about their suspicious neighbour, but the officers kept changing the subject. They told the couple that they needed to talk and ushered Cliff into a room while asking Wilma to take Syras and have a seat in the reception area. Wilma was frustrated; she didn't like how this visit was turning out. She had something to say, something she believed was of value to the investigation, and she'd been shut down, separated from Cliff and relegated to the waiting room. "Just when I thought I would explode, the two officers came out," Wilma writes in her book. The receptionist watched Syras, and Wilma was escorted to the room where her husband sat. The police officers excused themselves and left the room. It was just Cliff and Wilma in the room, alone. The weight of the situation had yet to set in.

Wilma knew something was wrong but couldn't figure out what that "something" might be. And then Cliff spoke. "They've found Candace…she's dead." At first Wilma couldn't accept the reality of those words. Even though in her heart she knew all along that Candace wasn't alive, the finality of that moment stunned her into disbelief. There was no longer any hope, however tentative, that their daughter would come home again. No longer any chance that their little family would be whole again. No possibility of being embarrassed in the media because of a daughter they thought was so well adjusted had actually run away. Candace was really that lovely young girl her parents portrayed to anyone who would listen. And her life had been cruelly taken; a senseless act of violence had destroyed a bright light.

The couple would later find out more details about their daughter's demise as the investigation continued, but at that moment, all Cliff told Wilma was that Candace had been found close to home, in a shack near the Nairn overpass, a scant 500 metres from the Derksens' home. Her hands and feet were bound behind her back by a thick rope. She wouldn't have been able to move. Although the young girl's body had only been discovered that very morning, and the autopsy still had to take place, the authorities believed Candace froze to death.

The Derksens later learned a little more about the scene where their daughter's body was found. They'd hear that the crime scene was disorganized, and that because Candace's vocal chords hadn't been swollen, it appeared she hadn't screamed. They'd know that their daughter had not been sexually assaulted; that if sex was a motivation in the attack, it had never progressed to that level. They'd know that aside from being bound, Candace hadn't been injured in any way. And, yes, their belief that their daughter was a virgin would be confirmed.

But at that moment, in the police station, Wilma struggled with the abbreviated version of the last moments of her daughter's life. She couldn't accept the truth of Cliff's words.

It was too weird—was it a bizarre coincidence that had brought them to the police station just after their daughter's body had been found, or was it an act of providence? Why hadn't the police called them earlier that day? When were the authorities planning on letting them know they'd found Candace? Nothing made any sense.

Cliff explained to his wife that the police had been trying to call David Loewen or Pastor Epp, the Derksens' pastor, because they didn't want the Derksens to find out without the support of their friends. Both men were out of town, so it made sense that the police weren't able to get in touch with them, and investigators hadn't yet decided on an alternative plan for breaking the sad news to the Derksens. It was at that point that the Derksens had arrived at the police station.

Everyone else, on the other hand, seemed to be aware of the discovery. The media was waiting for Candace's family to be notified before going public with the information. And when they did, an entire city went into mourning, and any thought that something like a stranger abduction couldn't happen in Winnipeg was extinguished, forever. ∾

Is This for Real?

The body was discovered by an Alsip's Industrial Products employee who had been looking for an old saw in a seldom-used shed on the company's Cole Avenue property. Although police were sure the body was that of the missing girl, Cliff and Wilma still had to make a positive identification. The drive to Seven Oaks Hospital, where Candace's body was being held, was a painfully solemn one. The medical examiner met the couple as they arrived at the front doors of the hospital and escorted them to a private room. In an effort to prepare the couple for what they were about to see, the medical examiner described the way Candace looked, and then showed them two photographs of the young girl. Wilma and Cliff now had an idea of what to expect, but it didn't make viewing the body any easier. In her book, Wilma described the scene at the hospital that day:

> They took us down an endless corridor, and someone held Syras while we went into a little white room. A tiny figure lay draped with a white sheet on what appeared to be an operating table.
>
> It wasn't Candace. In real life Candace was so much bigger. This was just a little corpse. But I forced myself to look closer. Yes, it was Candace. Candace minus her personality was so small, so terribly small, just a shell. Frozen, she looked like a grotesque, dusty mannequin, and I drew back in horror...It was Candace's body, but it wasn't Candace.

More than 2000 people turned up for Candace's funeral. During the service, Pastor Epp said, "Whatever evil befell Candace, it will not have the last word in her life. God's peace is the last word." The grieving had really begun. The Derksens no longer had any choice about developing a new "normal" for their family. Life without Candace was now a painful permanence. The family was flooded with cards and letters of condolences—as many as 40 per day—and it helped knowing how much people cared. And in some small way, the Derksens were vindicated. Anyone who'd followed the stories over the last two months now knew the Derksens were telling the truth about their daughter and their relationship with her. The investigation could get on with finding the stranger responsible for their pain.

However, exactly where the police were focusing their attention once again shocked the couple. It became clear that the authorities still hadn't made up their mind about the Derksens, or at the very least hadn't decided what they thought about Cliff. They'd questioned both parents the day before the funeral, asking them to write out statements and encouraging them to be specific. Wilma thought the timing of the request odd and noticed Cliff was irritated by the situation, but with a funeral on their minds, it was quickly forgotten.

Four months after Candace's death, Wilma learned through Lily Loewen, a co-worker with Camp Arnes, that the police did indeed have a suspect in her daughter's murder—Wilma's husband. This revelation didn't make any sense to Wilma. Cliff's whereabouts had been more than adequately accounted for on the day Candace didn't come home from school. He was at work until Wilma had picked him up, and over the next several days, the two were almost always together.

Lily went on to explain that the police had a theory. They thought that perhaps Cliff, during one of his evening excursions that first night when Candace went missing, had discovered his daughter in a "compromising" situation. Angry and wanting to drill home his displeasure at her behaviour, the police proposed that Cliff bound his daughter and put her in the shed where she was eventually discovered. Investigators didn't believe he had planned to kill her, just punish her. But when he went out to the shed later that night, she was dead. At that point, there was no turning back.

Wilma's head throbbed with the realization that the police were, in her estimation, wasting their time once again. They'd wasted their time thinking Candace was merely a runaway when, in fact, she was being held against her will and dying a slow death in a cold and lonely place. And they were again wasting their time investigating Cliff. Now that she knew what the police were thinking, bits and pieces of assorted events started to make sense to Wilma. Such as the time the police happened to pop by the Derksen home just after Cliff had received a telephone call from someone claiming to have information on Candace's death. The couple had always wondered about the coincidence; Wilma concluded that their phone could have been tapped. There was no other explanation. The realization infuriated her. A murderer was getting away while police were wasting their resources hounding an innocent man.

Wilma later found herself confronting her resentments and coming to terms with the knowledge that all too often someone close to a child abduction and murder is responsible for the crime, but for the time being she was shaken. Cliff was eventually interrogated and subjected to a polygraph test. He passed with flying colours, and the police ruled him out as a person of interest in Candace's abduction, but the pain of being a suspect in his own daughter's death wouldn't heal without a lot of prayer. The Derksens not only needed to work on forgiving a killer, but they also had to learn how to forgive the police as well. ᔥ

Moving On and Making Headway

Life challenges the living. Aside from a healthy period of grieving, and the occasional indulgence of tears we allow ourselves in the privacy of our own bedrooms, far away from public scrutiny, we have to compartmentalize our grief to some degree if we are to manage the demands of each day. Life doesn't stop— not even for a tragedy such as the one that befell the Derksens. Odia and Syras needed to feel safe and, for their benefit at the very least, that new and elusive "normal" way of living had to evolve. Bills had to be paid. Jobs required attention.

Cliff continued with his work at Camp Arnes. Wilma poured her energies into helping other families who were going through the aftermath of violence. Working with a group of volunteers, Wilma helped establish a Manitoba branch of the national group Child Find. She co-authored a guidebook to help families and loved ones of victims of violence work their way through their pain. She was also acting director of Victims' Voice, an organization whose goal is to support families of homicide victims.

In her book *Candace Is Missing! A True Story of Faith and Forgiveness* (1991), Wilma shared her horror of losing a child as a result of violence and described the faith that helped her through the ordeal. She followed up with the theme of forgiveness in two more books—*Unsettled Weather: How Do I Forgive?* and *Confronting the Horror: The Aftermath of Violence*. And just as Wilma and the rest of her family were coming to terms with the thought that Candace's killer might never be found, 22 years after her frozen body was discovered in a storage shed, an arrest was made.

On the morning of Wednesday, May 16, 2007, 43-year-old Mark Edward Grant was charged with first-degree murder in connection with the 1984 death of Candace Derksen. Police made the arrest based on DNA evidence found at the scene. Although investigators didn't elaborate on exactly what that evidence was, Inspector Tom Legge told reporters at a news conference that "a hair found near the frozen, confined body of the girl provided a break in the case." Grant lived in the area where Candace went missing, was known to police and was among the roughly 100 people interviewed in the early part of the investigation. Even though Grant had already exhibited criminal behaviour that could suggest he'd be capable of committing the kind of atrocity that befell young Candace, he was never considered a solid suspect at that time.

A more recent investigation into Grant's past paints the picture of an offender with a history of sexual assault and violent criminal offences. Grant spent the 13 years from 1991 to 2004 in prison. At one point, when he finally received parole, and during his nine days of relative freedom, he raped another woman. Parole board documents point out that Grant had an "established pattern of violent and sexually deviant behaviour dating back to 1983." On December 16, 2005, following Grant's release from prison, the Manitoba government posted a photograph of Grant on their sex offender notification webpage, warning all adult women and children of both sexes that coming into contact with Grant put them at risk of sexual violence.

Headlines of the arrest blared across the front pages of Winnipeg's dailies, newscasts reviewed the case and once again Cliff and Wilma were in front of the cameras. "Wilma and I have to admit that we had actually given up hope. We were already prepared to live with this mystery that has shadowed our family for so many years," Cliff told reporters in a prepared statement. "Now we have some answers and the promises of even more... We feel relief of the shadow...Justice is important. Finding truth and holding someone accountable for their actions re-establishes a sense of safety for us all..."

Following the announcement, Lianna McDonald, executive director of Child Find Manitoba, told Sun Media reporter

Chris Kitching that the arrest sends out a message of hope to all families mourning the loss of a murdered loved one and still looking for answers, awaiting justice and closure. "I think, secondly, it sends a message to those offenders or people who commit these types of crimes against children that their time will come, too."

It's been more than two years since Grant's arrest, and the Derksens are still waiting for justice and answers in their daughter's murder. As of the printing of this book, Grant has yet to appear before the courts. He is being held in custody and has been refused bail. Investigators are understandably tight-lipped about the case. Candace's family and the residents of Winnipeg will have to wait a bit longer to hear the answers they've been waiting for all these years.

Chapter Five

Down by the River—
Alexandra Wiwcharuk

Anyone who has been to Saskatoon will likely agree
that it's a pretty city. In the summer the city's streets
are rich with greenery, thickly lined with American
elm and varieties of ash, some of which date back to the earliest
days of this urban centre. And the meandering South Saskatchewan River not only adds character to the prairie city but also
divides the community into east and west, and the seven bridges
required to cross the river resulted in Saskatoon's nickname of
"Bridge City."

Although not everyone agrees with this next statement,
the largest city in Saskatchewan has also acquired a less than
desirable reputation of late. Figures released by Statistics Canada in 2007 reported that Saskatoon recorded an average of
1606 violent crimes per 100,000 residents annually, making it,
according to *Maclean's* magazine, a city whose crime rate ranks

"163 percent above the national average" and is, therefore, the "most dangerous city" in the country.

This certainly wasn't the case in 1962. Although the city was experiencing a period of rapid growth, Saskatoon was still very much a gentle prairie community with a population of 95,526, roughly half of what it is today. The majority of these residents were comprised of close-knit families who upheld long-standing, wholesome ideals. That in no way suggests the city didn't have its renegades, but ordinary folks didn't worry about their safety; any major criminal activities were the stuff of movies and organized crime.

In her book, *The Girl in Saskatoon*, Sharon Butala notes that between 1883—when the first Europeans settled in the area—and 1961, only 10 murders were committed in the city. And as Wilf Popoff, a former crime beat reporter with *The Star-Phoenix*, said in a 2004 interview about Saskatoon at that time, "the biggest thing you could do wrong was get caught for speeding."

And so it was that on the evening of Friday, May 18, 1962, the close of a particularly hot spring day in Saskatoon, 23-year-old Alexandra Wiwcharuk was strolling along the river-bed, enjoying her surroundings and not giving much thought to issues of safety. As the last of the sun's rays swept over the city and evening beckoned, Alexandra, or Alex, as her family called her, was just one of many people enjoying the outdoors. Near the train bridge, not too far from where Alex had stopped to enjoy the view, young boys were tossing a line in the river, hoping to snag the first pike or walleye of the year or, if they were lucky, a sturgeon, because back then it was still legal to pull the odd sturgeon from the South Saskatchewan. Motorists were cruising along nearby city streets, and as the business day wound down, the energy of the eve of the Victoria Day long weekend filled the air.

With the warmth the city was getting and the encouraging bright sunshine of the last few days, it wouldn't be long before the trees lining the majority of the South Saskatchewan River would be flush with new leaves. Alex continued on her way for a while, walking near the train bridge where most of the trees had been bulldozed, with the exception of a small clump of bushes clustered around a portable shack used by construction crews. But the ebb and flow of the water meandering along that winding river can be mesmerizing, so Alex decided to stop to drink it all in for a while.

She sat by the riverside with her arms wrapped around her knees and her chin resting on top. Perhaps she was thinking about her job at Saskatoon City Hospital, where she was scheduled to work the entire weekend. It was only natural that the recently graduated nurse, who had just started working at the hospital the September before, would pull duty for the first long-weekend of the summer. But the young woman still yearned for a weekend full of barbecues and picnics and time out with friends.

Alexandra probably noticed the boys with the fishing rods; perhaps she even saw one or the other wrestle with a tug on the line. She likely watched the small sparrows that, by now, were filling the air with their songs and flittering from treetops to grass and back to the trees again. She might have even watched a train or two make its way over the Railway Bridge. And maybe the sunset was red that evening, "a sailor's delight" promising clear skies for the next day. Whatever Alexandra was thinking or dreaming in those last hours of May 18 we'll never know, because there was one thing that Alexandra failed to notice, or at least did not notice in time to save herself. There was danger lurking nearby. ∾

WHERE'S ALEXANDRA?

In 1962, Alice Hall, Doreen Badduke and Pauline Tyllis shared a basement suite with Alexandra, and all four of the young women appeared to have had a busy day on May 18. Pauline had to work an evening shift that began at 3:00 PM, Alice was out looking at other apartments, and Doreen was getting ready for a night out, so none of them had spent a lot of time with Alex that day. Still, they all knew Alexandra wouldn't be out socializing that night. She'd slept most of the day, having worked the graveyard shift the evening before, and was scheduled for a shift at the hospital at 11:30 that night.

Alexandra woke earlier that afternoon, ate a light meal and wrote two letters—one to a sister in Thunder Bay, Ontario, and another to a friend in Calgary, Alberta. Alex then told Doreen that she planned to go for a walk outside their City Park apartment, located on Seventh Avenue North. She was going to stop at nearby Mead's Drugstore first, to mail her two letters, and after her walk she was going to return home and change before heading to work. The last time Doreen saw Alexandra was about 8:30 PM—she remembered the time because Doreen had just stopped by the apartment to pick up something. Ten minutes later Alice returned home after a visit with her landlady, but Alexandra had already left the apartment.

Alexandra never arrived at Saskatoon City Hospital that night. She didn't come home the next day. And no one had any clue where she might have gone.

By midnight, Alexandra's workmates from the hospital had already called her apartment twice. Her co-workers and supervisors knew Alex wouldn't be late without a good reason—something was definitely wrong when the punctual nurse missed work and hadn't called in to explain why. By morning, when Alex still hadn't returned home, her roommates were more than a little concerned. Alice told CBC's *The Fifth Estate* that her reaction to the situation was immediate and frightening. "I knew 100 percent that there was something very bad wrong." Pauline called the police. Someone contacted the Wiwcharuk family, asked them if they'd seen Alexandra and told them of her absence from work the night before. And a sense of malaise quickly settled over Alexandra's loved ones.

At first, the fact that nobody knew where Alexandra was didn't raise alarm bells with the police. They wouldn't get involved until the required 24 hours passed, and even then, the young nurse was treated as a missing person and her file was relegated to the morality division of the Saskatoon police department. After the initial 24-hour waiting period was over, the usual investigation unfolded, with police asking anyone who knew Alexandra if they'd seen her. But the Wiwcharuk family didn't wait to search. Like Alex's roommate, Alice, who knew right away that something was dreadfully wrong, the family knew their Alex was in trouble, and they immediately started combing the neighbourhood and contacting her friends and acquaintances. ∾

In the Beginning

Every child is special, but from the beginning, the Wiwcharuks knew Alexandra would do great things with her life. The young professional was an exemplary student and a hard worker. As the youngest of 10 children, Alex had six brothers and three sisters always looking out for her. Her siblings also taught the young girl everything they knew, and Alexandra thrived and flourished as any child would with such positive attention.

She was the only sibling to attend post-secondary school; her older siblings and her parents, who had farmed for four decades near the town of Endeavour, Saskatchewan, had saved enough money to see her through high school in Saskatoon and then college. Her parents pinned all their hopes and dreams for family success on the young woman, and she rose to the challenge.

Initially, Alexandra wanted to become a flight attendant—it would be a wonderful way to see all the dreamy and exotic places a young prairie girl at that time and place could only dream about seeing. But she was a petite young woman, measuring a slight 5-feet 1-inch tall, and she didn't meet the height requirements. Instead, Alexandra enrolled at the Yorkton Union Hospital School of Nursing in 1959 and graduated from the nurse's training program in 1961.

She was also a stunning woman; photographs depict a dreamy-eyed beauty with full lips and dark hair that appeared to have a natural wave to it. Every image shows her with her head held high and shoulders back, drawing attention to her long, lean neck and giving her a regal quality. It's no wonder she was publicly recognized for her beauty and grace, earning the title of Queen of the Kinette Skating Carnival in Yorkton in 1960, and then again when she was chosen to represent the city in the Saskatchewan Wheat Queen contest that same year.

In 1961, Alexandra's photo was submitted without her knowledge to a beauty contest with a twist. A Saskatchewan radio station requested photos from young women of the province who were interested in becoming "The Girl in Saskatoon." Johnny Cash himself, the author of the song and budding superstar, was coming to Saskatoon on tour and was scheduled to perform at a local fair. One source suggests the contest was his idea, and the lucky woman to land the title was in for a treat. Alexandra was shocked when, after being called up on stage and serenaded in front of 1500 of Johnny Cash's adoring fans, she was named "The Girl in Saskatoon."

In short, Alexandra was a woman who knew she was loved by the people she valued most, had earned a degree and had landed the job of her dreams. She wasn't the kind of young woman to wilfully abscond from her life. She wouldn't disappear on a lover's tryst or abandon her responsibilities. And her family loved her; she'd never do anything to tarnish her reputation in their eyes.

Sadly, society in the 1960s often typecast young women who didn't follow what some deemed was a set prescription for adulthood; namely, she was 23 and still single. That was tantamount to being a spinster, but that wasn't likely for Alexandra. Someone with her looks surely had suitors. This could only mean she was single by choice—which likely raised questions among some folks who didn't know her. Was she the kind of woman who liked to date a lot of different men?

People who knew her, of course, rejected any dishonourable suggestions about their Alex. They knew what kind of person she was, and they weren't about to allow her to be pigeonholed by the public or the police. Her family certainly wasn't going to stand by without making darn sure the police were doing everything in their power to find her. According to one news report, shortly after Alexandra disappeared, her brother Mike and a few other family members "stormed the police station and confronted Police Chief Jim Kettles." Alex's behaviour wasn't what anyone would expect from her—Mike remembered drilling the fact home to the police chief. "We told him, 'Hey, this is not like Alexandra.'"

Aside from making routine phone calls and asking questions, it wasn't until Wednesday, May 23, that the police made the first of two concrete and overt efforts to find the young woman. A Saskatoon police officer owned a dog and, taking the advice of an RCMP dog handler, was training his pet in police dog techniques. The officer took the dog on a search of the riverbank but came up with nothing other than a discarded tissue that investigators thought might have belonged to Alexandra. A few days later, on May 28, thinking perhaps the young woman might have fallen into the river, police boats were launched, and investigators cruised for about 41 kilometres downstream from the Railway Bridge, looking for anything that might suggest what had become of Alex. Nothing.

By now, the local media were carrying stories about the missing woman, so it seemed odd that a strange observation went unchecked for a time. Three boys had been playing alongside the river, and one of the bunch, who was particularly intent on digging up some worms to use for fish bait, had apparently stumbled on what seemed to be a hand reaching from the earth.

One of the boys told his uncle who was fishing nearby, but he must not have been paying attention. Perhaps he didn't believe the youngsters. Or maybe he just didn't want to take the time away from his fishing. Whatever the reason, the man dismissed the boys and continued casting his line.

About a week later, the young lads were still unable to get what they'd seen out of their mind, and so they talked their three older, female cousins into going to see what they'd found. The girls, shocked and frightened, rushed back home to tell of the discovery. It was enough to convince the man, who was later identified in news reports as Andrew Pschetter, to follow his nephew, his two sons and the girls to the only clump of trees still standing in that area. At 9:00 PM, on May 31, Pschetter called police, telling them what the boys had found—a body, buried in the riverbank "about 50 feet east of the intersection of 33rd Street and Spadina Crescent, and about 100 feet from the water's edge." It wasn't what the Wiwcharuk family had hoped for, but it was the answer they had dreaded. The baby girl who'd blossomed into a beautiful young woman was dead, her body carelessly discarded like it was nothing more than kitchen waste, a mere 730 metres from her home. ∾

BAD NEWS GETS WORSE

If the knowledge that Alexandra was dead didn't just about destroy her dad, Alexander, mother, Anna, and her entire family, learning of the circumstances surrounding her death was beyond comprehension. As soon as the police unearthed the woman's remains, it was clear she'd been horribly violated in almost every way. She was naked from the waist down, her pants and underwear cinched around her right ankle. Her shirt and bra had been ripped open and, as Butala notes in her book, "her knees were still flexed and her legs spread when she was found."

But Alexandra had experienced even more humiliation and abuse before she died. Her nose was broken, and one of her eyes was black and swollen. Her skull had been bludgeoned; some reports suggest the seven-centimetre thick, five-kilogram slab of concrete someone had heaved on Alexandra's chest before burying her caused the damage to her skull, but the lack of blood on the object left investigators questioning the possibility. The beating likely rendered her unconscious—surely God in His mercy would have made it so—but it did not kill her. Alex had been buried alive, and the soil and sand clogging her nasal passages, her mouth and her airways signified that she had suffocated to death.

According to an article dated June 2, 1962, Saskatoon's police chief, Jim Kettles, said he believed Alexandra's body was dumped in a "natural depression in the bluff, the only one around for at least a quarter of a mile, then covered with dirt." He didn't think Alexandra was killed elsewhere and then dumped; in his view the crime took place near or where the body was discovered. If that was the case, surely someone noticed the altercation, or at least heard the young woman's screams. And she must have screamed, because the skin collected from her fingernails gave the impression she'd put up a wild fight for her life. It also seemed strange that none of the construction workers, who had likely passed by the haphazardly buried body frequently in the intervening time between Alexandra's murder and the discovery of her body, noticed anything. She was buried in plain sight, as though the murderer wanted her to be found, and yet no one noticed anything until three little boys happened along.

The area was immediately cordoned off; almost two weeks had passed since her disappearance, and police were anxious to sift through the area and collect whatever possible evidence they could still find. Along with her clothing and the body itself, police collected the slab of cement found on her chest, a brick, three empty beer bottles and many dark reddish-brown hairs. It was later discovered that the hairs belonged to Alexandra so weren't useful in identifying a murderer.

When Kettles spoke to the media, he said the violence perpetrated against Alexandra was the worst thing he'd ever seen in his career as a police officer, and he appealed to the public, asking anyone who'd been in the area of Mead's Drugstore and the Railway Bridge on Friday, May 18, to try to remember if they'd seen Alexandra or noticed anything out of the ordinary. The public, equally horrified by what they were reading in their local newspapers, clamoured to come forward.

Police learned through the pharmacy apprentice at Mead's, who thought Alexandra had come to the drugstore sometime between 8:00 PM and 8:30 PM, that the beautiful young nurse seemed to be in a good mood. Dressed in green pants, a colourful blouse and a dark green sweater, the apprentice remembered sharing a joke with Alexandra and that she had laughed.

At some point, police heard from a young husband and father who, after working late that night, noticed Alexandra on his drive home. Because of the direction in which she was walking, it was believed to be sometime after she'd mailed her letters. The man said Alexandra was talking to a tall, dark-haired gentleman who, it appeared, was overly dressed for a riverside stroll in his brown suit and white shirt, and the scene concerned the witness for some inexplicable reason. But he was late, already long past his dinner hour, and he had a family waiting for him at home, so he had continued on his way.

It appears the classy-looking gentleman didn't accompany Alexandra for long, because the boy who was fishing at the weir that night noticed her sitting on the concrete apron not far from the bridge itself. She was alone and clearly visible from most angles, and this led some investigators to speculate that perhaps she was planning to meet someone there and wanted to be seen.

Not far away, a 15-year-old boy was prodding his buddy to go with him to talk to the lone woman. The buddy was the shyer of the two and pressed his friend to go with him to nearby Mead's—he wanted to distract his outgoing partner from his desire to speak with the young woman so had pretended he was in the mood for a snack. In the half hour or so that the boys were away on their snack run, both Alexandra and the boy fishing nearby had left. The young buddy breathed a sigh of relief.

Later that night, a group of young men drove past the area, and after a few too many beers, needed to empty their bladders. They told police that they pulled over near the river to do just that, but didn't notice anything.

One by one, a concerned public, forever changed by the violence in their midst, called investigators with whatever bits of information they had. The boy fishing on the weir that night was identified as 16-year-old Billy McGaffin and, after undergoing hypnosis by Saskatoon doctor Lewis Brand at the request of officer Hugh Fraser, police heard about another person sitting alone on the apron. McGaffin thought Alex left the riverbank around 10:00 PM, and he remembered seeing two cars parked nearby on Spadina Crescent: one was a red, sporty car, and the other was an older "Ford-type" car. Police tested McGaffin, asking him about Alex's shoes, and the boy described them accurately. Because that bit of information was one of the things kept from the public, the police were interested in what McGaffin had to say. But was he a witness or a perpetrator?

The small pieces of information that trickled into the media over the years were often inconsistent. Were there two or three boys who found Alexandra? Was there only one teenage boy fishing nearby when Alexandra sat beside the bridge, or were there more? Was a son from a prominent family a suspect in the murder, or was it simply that the person of interest had a similar name as that family? Was this vicious crime the act of a single offender, or was there more than one individual involved? And why in heaven's name were people so silent? How can something so vile happen in the open and no one have seen anything?

Word on the street was that a "local doctor" might have been somehow involved in the murder, or perhaps it was the son of a politician; however, both men were cleared of any involvement early on in the murder investigation.

At one point, Canada's notorious serial killer, Clifford Olson, was considered a possible suspect in the case. There were some similarities to Alexandra's murder and some of Olson's victims, but there appeared to be confusion around exactly where he was at the time of the murder. One news story suggested he was in Saskatoon, having just been released from a Prince Albert jail, whereas another source said he was still incarcerated at the time of Alex's death.

Alexandra's boyfriend, Hugh Carlton, was questioned shortly after arriving in Waskesiu with his buddies for a weekend of lakeside fun. According to Alice, Hugh had called that Friday night asking for Alexandra and saying he wanted to offer her a ride to work. Perhaps knowing that she was scheduled to work that weekend, he wanted to spend what scant few moments he could with his girlfriend before continuing on with his buddies. But Alice told him Alex was out, and Hugh reportedly left town without getting a chance to say goodbye.

Hugh eventually became a police officer. He told *The Fifth Estate* that he always found the crime odd in that no other sexually motivated crimes had been reported in the province that he knew of, nor any sadistically based murders. "I would have thought there would have or should have been more crimes [of that nature]," he said to reporter Linden MacIntyre. A crime filled with this degree of rage—and surely some kind of rage was involved to motivate such powerful destruction to a human body—doesn't sound like the work of a single-victim murderer. Unless, of course, it was motivated by extreme passion. Either way, Hugh was never able to shed any light on his girlfriend's homicide. Like his colleagues on the force, he's still haunted by the crime.

Aside from Hugh, Alexandra had another caller that Friday night. Alice told the coroner's inquest that another man had phoned that same night. He was trying to set up a double date with Alex for the following evening. That wasn't surprising. A lot of men seemed to be interested in dating Alex or in keeping her close by as a good friend. Was it possible that some of the gentlemen she turned down felt unduly spurned by her rejection? Could her murderer have been a slighted admirer? Or was he a secret admirer who watched and followed her from a distance, waiting for the right time to make his move?

In one newspaper story, Kettles told reporters that the city's entire complement of officers, all 131 of them, were investigating the case at one point. Within the first two months, 52 persons of interest were interviewed and eliminated as possible suspects. It was a good thing that some progress was being made in the case, because it seemed as though there was no end to the people who might have been involved in Alexandra's murder.

Today, her file contains 1100 names, and cold-case detective Sergeant Phil Farion, who as of this writing was assigned to the case, says he believes the name of the killer is on that list. It's a matter of narrowing down those names, and each suspect needs to be thoroughly investigated before moving on to the next one. It's an incredibly time-consuming process. And today, almost 50 years later, it's a case that remains unsolved. ◦∾

Science, and Family, Lend a Hand

Alexandra Wiwcharuk had many young nieces, aged three to 11 years old, and the girls often talked about the auntie they missed and how when they got older they'd help the police solve the crime. Since 1992, four of those nieces, Lynn Gratix, Lorain Phillips, Patty Storie and Gwen Taralson, have been carrying on an investigation of their own into their aunt's murder. Initially they travelled to Saskatoon every few years, visiting the area where Alex was last seen and talking to folks who still lived there and remembered their aunt.

As with every violent case, the police worked hard over the years to bring a murderer to justice, but flaws and inconsistencies appeared in the investigation—at least from a layperson's point of view with the admittedly limited information available to someone outside of law enforcement. Most importantly, no one has been brought to justice for this terrible crime. Whether the killer is still alive or has since passed away isn't as important to Alex's nieces as the need to hold someone accountable for the murder, even if posthumously. And maybe in the process, they will get answers to the questions surrounding a mystery that has haunted their family for almost five decades.

"Ultimately, we want to help solve this crime," Storie told *The Fifth Estate*. "We want to help the police with whatever information we can come up with and pass it on to them and ultimately we want the case solved for our family—we want closure for our family."

Certainly, the key people who could have provided valuable information have died since 1962, and the details of memory fade. Even so, the four women searching for justice for their aunt have conducted many interviews with friends, acquaintances and anyone who was in any way connected with Alex's story, and they've collected boxes full of evidence. In some instances, people have been more forthright with these women than they have been with the police.

"We have found that, in some of our interviews that we have all conducted, that a lot of people have come to us and said…'we've never wanted to talk to the police because we're kind of scared to approach them'…they just find that we're more approachable," Storie said.

Then there's the concept of space and time. As Lynn Gratix added, "Everybody's aged…and they don't feel as scared, 'cause back then they were scared of the police or even saying something 'cause what if that murderer was out there…it's their time to come out and speak."

And it is time for people to open up; the gentle poking and prodding of these brave women has yielded results. Along with their boxes of evidence, one of the nieces has "legally" collected a DNA sample. They've also devised four working theories on what could have happened that night in 1962. The theories involve five possible suspects, four of whom are still alive. And in June 2008, when asked if they believe the person responsible was still alive, Storie told Darren Bernhardt of *The StarPhoenix*, "Persons [and] Yes."

Alex's family isn't the only one still delving into the mystery of her death. In the 1990s, police dug out the evidence collected from the scene and hoped the science of the day, considerably more developed than it was in the 1960s, would yield some clues. Sadly, it was not to be. Some of the material wasn't stored properly, and the samples had been compromised. Other pieces of evidence were either lost or stolen. This has left the police with very little to work with.

In 2004, Saskatoon's cold-case detectives exhumed Alexandra's body for possible DNA evidence. Miraculously, foreign hairs were discovered. Initially, those hairs were sent to the RCMP crime lab in Regina, but the technology there wasn't able to provide a profile. The samples were then forwarded to Molecular World Inc., in Thunder Bay, Ontario. According to its website, Molecular World Inc. is "the only SCC [Standards Council of Canada] Accredited facility in Canada that specializes and provides services in all three technologies (STR, Y-STR and Mitochondrial DNA) required for Human Identification." Their technological abilities allow them to test everything from saliva to semen, blood, teeth and hair.

It appears the lab was as good as its word; it was successful in producing a DNA profile. Their findings also suggested that more than one person could have been involved in Alex's rape and murder. Perhaps the four nieces were on to something, with their theory that the murder involved more than one individual.

Cold-case detective Sergeant Phil Farion said that in 2008, police had chosen 13 persons of interest from among the 1100 names in Alex's file and were matching the DNA profile against these individuals. It's a time-consuming process, and investigators had to select where they'd begin ruling out suspects. Another thing that had to be considered was that the hair discovered in the 2004 exhumation could very well have belonged to the undertaker; nothing is a sure thing when it comes to investigating a murder.

In October 2008, Alex's nieces erected a billboard in Saskatoon's downtown core. A portion of the billboard displays a stunning, formal photograph of Alexandra and the words "Nurse MURDERED 1962" emblazoned across the top, along with her name, the website address dedicated to her memory and a phone number for tips underneath. Her nieces are hopeful that someone who may know something about the case might still live in that city, and that seeing the image of an innocent victim who died a horrible death will stir that person's heart enough to talk. No bit of information is too small or insignificant for the police and the Wiwcharuk family.

The clock is still ticking, but in a sense, time has stood still for Alexandra's loved ones. They will not rest. Like other family members of the victims of violent crime, Alex's death so many years ago has forever defined their present and their future. Nothing will ever be the same again, but things can be better.

When *The Fifth Estate* asked the four nieces whether they were serious about their research, if they really thought they'd be instrumental in solving the case, Lorain said, "Absolutely…It's because it is such a violent crime to have hurt her body like that, to have raped her, to have buried her alive and then just get away with it! No way…not only is it my auntie, this is my duty."

Should their quest not produce a resolution as quickly as they would hope, and Gwen, Lynn, Lorain and Patty have reached an age where they can't continue their search, another generation of Wiwcharuks is willing to carry on.

Alex was too important to them to forget her pain. Justice is too important to let a killer remain free.

Chapter Six

Into the Void—Charles Horvath

When trekking through the wilderness, the silence is sometimes so thick it numbs the senses, and for a moment you can't hear your feet touching the ground. The sinuous whine of a motorboat, the sour smell of car exhaust on a hot summer's day, the sounds of horns honking or elevator music pumping into shopping malls and grocery stores are mere memories. And then a gust of wind comes up, and the heave and yawn of a ponderosa pine, towering a dozen or more metres skyward, shatters the silence. The moment grounds you in a different kind of reality.

Kelowna is nestled in the Okanagan Valley along Okanagan Lake and surrounded by wilderness trails that veer off into the wall of hills that surrounds the interior British Columbian valley. Within a few minutes drive from Kelowna's city centre a person can find themselves lost in wilderness bliss, hiking up Black Mountain maybe, scaling the fire tower and looking down

over one of British Columbia's most popular summer destinations. Blueberries and Saskatoon berries grow abundantly on
these hillsides, and their pulp, made ready by a hot and brilliant
Okanagan sun, are sweeter and more flavourful than anything
you'll ever buy at your local market. Family orchards dotting
the valley sell cherries, peaches and other fair-weather produce
by the bucketful. And if you prefer your fruit fermented, the
area is home to several world-class wineries.

Natural beauty aside, Okanagan beaches are a magnet
for all kinds of water-sport enthusiasts. While jet skiers criss-
cross their way along Okanagan Lake, water skiers time each
other on the slalom course, and wind surfers silently slice their
way across the water. These days you can't fish for kokanee, but
you can still pull two trout a day—enough to grill up for a nice
dinner. And if you like to party the night away—well, Kelowna
has no shortage of dance clubs and nightlife hotspots.

That's the picture of Kelowna today. The downtown has
had a bit of a facelift, but not that much has changed since 1989,
when 20-year-old Charles Horvath, a resident of England, first set
his eyes on the summer city and decided to stay a while. The
previous September, Denise Horvath-Allan gave her son an open-
ended ticket to Canada. Charles wanted to get to know everything
he could about the country of his birth and had planned to spend
the year working and backpacking his way from the east to the
west coast. He'd worked for several months in Montréal, Québec,
before heading on to the Ontario communities of Thunder Bay,

where he stopped for a brief visit with his father, Max, and then to Cochenour where he visited with his godfather. From there he alternately rode the bus and hitchhiked his way through Ontario and across the prairies, getting a taste for a smattering of the communities along the way and eventually stopping in Swift Current to cash a cheque at the Royal Bank. From there it was off to Banff, where he worked for a time before setting out one final time, on May 3, and arriving in the warm and radiant Okanagan. Life was good. Life was very good.

Denise looked forward to Charles' routine notes and phone calls, hearing him tell of the people he'd met and the adventures he'd had. These days the Internet would make that kind of communication very simple, but in 1989, Charles had to work hard to keep in touch. With a time difference of eight hours or more, depending on where he was in the country, phoning wasn't always convenient. Regular mail took too long, so Charles and his mother took to faxing each other. It was the most efficient way to stay in touch, especially when time was of the essence.

On May 11, Charles had a lot to tell his mother. His mom was making arrangements for that coming August. It was Charles' champagne birthday on the 21st, and Denise would be turning 40 a few days earlier: milestone birthdays for both of them and plans for a special celebration had been in the works for months. Charles initially wanted Denise and her second husband, Stuart, to meet him in Canada for their joint celebration, and then he talked about returning to England, even if he could only get a week off work. He could handle the jet lag if it meant being there to wish his mom a happy 40th. But eventually the two settled on meeting in Hong Kong. Denise's father, a British naval officer, had been stationed there throughout much of Denise's youth, and she was excited to show her son the places she used to go and the things she liked to do. It was turning into a season for reliving their roots.

But a Hong Kong rendezvous produced its own problems. After carefully researching flight costs from Vancouver, Charles was a little worried about earning the money he'd need for his ticket, but he had a plan. In a detailed fax that he sent to his mother from Kelowna's Roche Stationers, Charles shared his concerns about the cost of the flight, and he also told Denise of his efforts to get a lucrative job. Charles had registered at the student employment agency and had already picked up work here and there, laying carpet, doing irrigation work and digging turf at a family orchard. He even spent some time working at the Flintstones Theme Park. But he had his eye on something that would make him some serious cash—a job drilling and blasting. Charles was determined to make that Hong Kong trip.

"My 40th was important to him…he would have never missed that birthday," Denise remembered. "He kept saying, 'Mom, you're 40 on the 17th, and life begins at 40.'"

Although Denise would have lent Charles whatever he needed to make the trip, she'd already spent quite a lot of money on his Canadian excursion, and she was grateful for Charles' efforts to raise the money for his plane ticket.

It was the last time Denise heard from her son.

At first, she didn't worry. Charles was a big boy. At a towering six feet in height and weighing about 175 pounds, he didn't exactly look like someone who needed protection—or his mother doting over him. After all, the lad had joined the French Foreign Legion when he was just 17. Surely he could take care of himself. Still, despite her efforts to reassure herself, by the end of May, Denise was worried enough to put a call through to the Kelowna RCMP.

"I was quite embarrassed, really, calling the RCMP, but I was so anxious waiting for Charles to make contact," she remembers. "I knew something was wrong and could not understand why Charles had not made contact so I could book the plane tickets from the UK to Hong Kong and Vancouver to Hong Kong. I was demented with worry. I kept telephoning his godfather and father to see if they had heard from Charles, but they hadn't. Had we not been arranging where we would meet up for our birthdays, I would not have been so anxious so soon after receiving his last letter by fax on May 11."

But Denise was worried. Her only child, her companion throughout the last 20 years, had suddenly lost touch with his mother. She knew something was wrong. ❧

IN THE BEGINNING

Northern Ontario is a vast expanse of rugged wilderness where the moose and bear population likely outnumber its human inhabitants. The municipality of Red Lake is in one of the more remote reaches of Sunset Country, a full 280 kilometres north of Kenora and the TransCanada Highway that wends its way through the craggy landscape making up much of Ontario's lake country. Population in the municipality's six communities of Red Lake, Madsen, Starrat-Olson, Balmertown, Cochenour and McKenzie Island blossomed after gold was discovered in the area in 1925. By 1926, an influx of Europeans had settled in the area, and mining was still among the area's most prominent industries when Max Horvath and his young wife Denise settled there in 1968. The two had met the year earlier, had married on December 28, 1967, and, like any young couple in love, they were enthralled with the endless possibilities that lay before them.

It was in the community of Cochenour that Karoly ("Charles" in Hungarian) John Horvath was born. Denise battled through a trying pregnancy and had a difficult delivery bringing her special treasure into the world. "For many months prior to the birth of Charles we had been planning to go to live in England mainly because of my ill health in the pregnancy," Denise explained.

Finally, about a month after Charles' birth, the young family was ready to make the move back to Yorkshire, England.

There, Denise would have the love and support of her mother and extended family, Max would most certainly find work, and they'd be able to start building their dreams.

When Denise and Max landed in Manchester, immigration officers stamped on Max's Certificate of Identity a limited visa even though arrangements had been made in Canada for the family to live in the UK permanently. "We sent the Certificate of Identity into the Foreign Office for a renewal of the visa which they did, but they stamped in the Certificate of Identity that Max must leave the UK two months before the Certificate of Identity [was supposed to have] expired."

On June 20, 1969, a discouraged Max flew out of Manchester and returned to Canada, leaving his wife and 10-month-old baby behind. Denise and Charles joined him in December 1970, and the couple earnestly tried to make a go of their marriage, but it was not to be. Within six weeks of their reunion, the couple separated, and the following September, Denise and Charles returned to England alone.

From that point on, it had always been the two of them. Denise and Charles. The mother and son duo grew to share a special bond. Given the choice, this was a path Denise probably would not have taken, but she made the best of being a single mother: Charles was the energy that gave her life meaning. She did everything she could to make a good life for him, which included maintaining a relationship with Max for her son's benefit. They discussed such things as Charles' education, and at times Charles would visit Canada and reacquaint himself with his father and extended Canadian family. That's what he was doing when he started his cross-Canada trek. He arrived in Montréal in September 1988. Denise met her handsome son in December and proudly watched him make his way down the catwalk of a fashion show on the 14th of that month. Charles and Denise celebrated the holidays early, and four days later, the mother and son shared a teary farewell as Denise returned to England.

Early in 1989, Charles started making his way to Ontario. He must have felt that he was travelling too heavy because he left his skis, duvet and formal clothing at his godfather's home in Cochenour. By the time he left Banff, he'd lost more of his luggage, this time because some of his belongings were stolen at the bus station there. He arrived in Kelowna with his pack considerably lightened but still equipped with a tent, clothing and a few personal items. Luggage, no luggage, partial luggage, jobs that didn't quite pan out the way he'd hoped and living accommodations that often fell flat—there were many ups and downs on the trip.

But it was the adventure of a lifetime, and no matter where Charles was, one thing about his trip remained consistent: he always connected with his mother. Even without the added need to correspond and iron out their August birthday plans, Charles always wrote or called home, telling Denise where he was working or living or asking for a few extra dollars when money was low. The mother and son were extremely close. The loss of communication was extremely odd.

"Had I still been a single parent, I would have been on that plane within weeks [of our last correspondence]—way before August 1989 [when Charles was reported officially missing]," Denise said. "I knew something was terribly wrong." In those first few days after Denise lost contact with Charles, Stuart was more inclined to believe that Charles would surprise Denise at home one day. After all, boys will be boys, and any number of things could have distracted Charles' attention away from his mother. Perhaps he'd fallen in love or was just really enjoying himself. Or maybe he had landed that perfect job, and it took him away from the convenience of phone and fax.

Even the police initially brushed aside Denise's concerns. They told her Charles was over 18. If he didn't want to call his mother, he didn't have to. They, too, believed a young man could be deterred from calling home for any number of reasons and were quick to point out that it had only been a few weeks between the time Charles sent his last fax home on May 11 and when Denise first contacted the RCMP—an initial contact that didn't even result in a file on Charles' case. In the eyes of the officials, no one was missing. There was nothing wrong.

The weeks passed. Their August birthdays passed. With still no word from her son, Denise's worry went into overdrive. "I just cried and cried. I knew something was terribly wrong," Denise said. "As the months passed...I was deranged with worry. When the letters I sent Charles were returned from General Delivery, Kelowna to the UK, with the odd bits of money I'd sent still in them, I just did not know what to do."

Police, in the meantime, were still leery about taking Denise's concerns seriously, despite extended family members echoing her worries about Charles' well-being. And with no one looking for her son, Denise was painfully aware that the trail leading to his whereabouts grew colder by the minute. Memories fade, especially where a new acquaintance is involved. Evidence gets destroyed. Denise couldn't help but think that investigators were losing valuable time.

From her home in England, Denise could do little more than worry and feel increasingly helpless. Her heart was fixed on deciding when and how she could go to Canada to search for her child, but she had no option but to stay in England and supervise the remodelling of her hair and beauty salon until it was complete. She did everything in her power to expedite the work at the salon while simultaneously calling the police in Canada, sending updated photographs of Charles and calling every family member in Canada that she could think of. Once renovations were completed, Denise secured a manager to run the site and was ready to fly to Canada. But not before a freak occurrence sent her reeling with emotion.

A few people in Denise's circle, trying to comfort her as best they could, suggested that Charles might in fact be out on a lark and would show up one day with a kid and wife in tow. "I hoped beyond imagination that Charles would," Denise said.

And then one day he did…or rather someone who looked a lot like Charles happened along. It was the spring of 1990. Denise and Stuart were at their Sowerby home when the Charles look-alike walked up to their front door.

"One evening, it was still daylight, the doorbell rang. I turned around to look out of the living room window and screamed, 'Charles is home!'" Denise remembers it like it was yesterday. "I ran to the door and to my dismay it was my beauty therapist with her boyfriend—he was Greek and had the same colouring as Charles. I ended up in a ball, hysterical under the stairs. It was at this stage Stuart realized how traumatized I was… it was agreed that I would go to Canada to look for my son myself."

Long before Denise set foot on Canadian soil for her first personal search for Charles in June 1990, plans were already being set in motion. If the police weren't going to get the word out about her son's disappearance, this mom-turned-sleuth certainly would. She'd already placed ads in the Red Lake newspaper in Ontario, the *Banff Crag & Canyon* and the *Kelowna Daily Courier*.

On her arrival in Kelowna, Denise placed more ads in the newspapers she'd already contacted, along with some in the *Kelowna Capital News* and the *Interior Buy & Sell*. She was now filled with a mixture of fear and adrenaline, anxious to get on with her search, visiting some of the places she knew Charles frequented and asking anyone who would listen if they knew her son. Stuart travelled with Denise to Canada that first trip, and Charles' grandparents, who arrived the next month, were also on hand to lend their support. Denise was also garnering interest from many of Kelowna's residents. But she still felt very much alone.

Almost without exception, she thought the police, the people who could help her the most, were discouraging her early efforts. Denise remembers one officer saying, "It is the belief of this detachment that your son is dead, we may never find out what happened to him or find his body." It might have deflated her for a time, but before long, the newspaper ads she'd placed were starting to do their job, and tips were coming in. It was enough to boost her energies and keep her focused on the task at hand. ∾

MISSING FRIEND

Joanne Zebroff didn't even know Charles was missing until her mom noticed the ad Denise placed in Kelowna's *Daily Courier* in June 1990. Had Joanne and her mother not read the ad, they might have missed learning about Charles' plight altogether. Denise had sent two photographs to the local papers, one with Charles sporting a beard and one with him clean-shaven. The paper used the bearded photo, and because Charles hadn't worn a beard during his time in Kelowna, the Zebroffs didn't recognize him by the photograph. They did, however, recognize his birth name: Karoly John Horvath.

By now, Denise was getting accustomed to the RCMP's repeated suggestions that Charles may have intentionally gone missing in an effort to get away from his life at the time and sort things out. Although their lack of interest in Charles' case eventually garnered vocal criticism from the people who knew him, others argued that the police weren't entirely out of line.

According to a 2005 consultation paper from the Policing, Law Enforcement and Interoperability Branch of Public Safety and Emergency Preparedness, about 100,000 people go missing in Canada every year. In many of these cases, the adults involved have left of their own accord, often because they just needed a break from the stresses of their lives. But of those who've intentionally disappeared, most return home within a month. Clearly, this wasn't the case with Charles.

"Of course he could run away...we can all do anything, but we usually need a reason and what reason did he have?" Denise asked. She went on to provide proof of the loving relationship she had with Charles through a plethora of photographs, but for the Kelowna police, it wasn't completely convincing. When Joanne and her mother came out of the woodwork saying they knew Charles, it was the first time someone other than Denise and Charles' immediate family had come forward with any kind of information on the young man. The stories Joanne and her mother shared with Denise reinforced what Denise had said all along—Charles loved his family and wouldn't have left and cut ties with her of his own accord.

In a letter, Joanne told Denise she first met Charles in the spring of 1989. He was walking along the street, and the two quickly struck up a conversation. It wasn't long before Joanne learned that Charles was from England and was making his way across Canada. Because Joanne had travelled through Europe in a similar fashion, she knew what it was like to need a bed to lay one's weary head and, after asking her mother's permission, she invited Charles to use the sofa for a night or two.

The next morning, Joanne's mother, Chris, dropped Charles off at a local carpet-fitting business where Charles had already secured a job with carpet-fitter Vernon Gordon through the job mart. Denise later discovered it was Gordon who suggested Charles check into the Tiny Town Tent and Trailer Campground after finding Charles sleeping on the floor on site and discovering he really didn't have a place to stay.

Although Charles only stayed at the Zebroffs' apartment for a couple of days, Joanne said the new friendship flourished, and Charles would pop by from time to time for a visit. The two had even taken an excursion together, hitchhiking to the O'Keefe Ranch in Vernon at one point. Joanne said Charles spoke only well of his family and talked of his excitement over the coming birthday celebrations planned for Hong Kong. She also described Charles as a bit of a storyteller, and she couldn't always believe what he said about his life of affluence in England

and his time serving in the French Foreign Legion. In fact, some of his stories could be quite annoying, and Joanne didn't have any problem telling him so. When he stopped showing up at her apartment, Joanne thought he'd likely moved on. After all, "any young man with a backpack and a tent—well, he can travel anywhere," Joanne later told interviewers from *Unsolved Mysteries*.

Still, despite his outlandish tales, Joanne felt she had a good sense of Charles. In a letter to *Unsolved Mysteries*, she'd describe him as "a braggart, a little lonely, trying to sort himself out, and simply here in Kelowna when summer momentum begins to set in." But as far as Joanne could see, Charles was happy, not at all the potential suicide victim some authorities had at one time suggested, and not someone who wanted to get away from his family. "I remember him always talking well of you," Joanne told Denise on several occasions. Joanne would likely never know how profoundly her words touched Denise's heart. Denise felt vindicated.

Beginning with Joanne's correspondence and the subsequent discussions they had in person, Denise was able to piece together Charles' movements throughout the month of May 1989. "We believe that Charles stayed at the Kelowna City Park on Wednesday, May 3, the Gospel Mission from Thursday May 4 to Saturday the 6th, then stayed at the Zebroffs on Sunday, May 7, and Monday, May 8, then slept on site where he was carpet fitting," Denise said, adding that Charles then spent a couple of days with Gordon before moving on to the campsite for the first time, sometime around May 11. Charles then faxed Denise on May 11, saying he had a couple of good job prospects and was waiting to hear about them. One job in particular, involving drilling and blasting, could fetch him $3000 per month—clearly enough to pay for his ticket to Hong Kong and keep him fairly comfortable during the rest of his trek.

Denise then learned that a few days later, possibly on May 14, Charles met up with Drew and Libby Sherwood, and in exchange for Charles helping them move into their new home, the couple invited him to stay in their guest cabin for a few nights. The Sherwoods echoed Joanne's experience of Charles, saying he was very friendly, loved to tell stories and perhaps verged on the naïve. As far as Denise could ascertain, Charles booked into the campground again around May 17 and paid for two nights. The Sherwoods enjoyed Charles' company, and some time around May 21, Drew drove Charles to a local orchard that was looking for fruit pickers and offered workers accommodations. "We don't know where he slept the following week," Denise said. Regardless what Charles' plans were, the Sherwoods had every expectation that they'd hear from him again. They considered him a friend, and when he didn't stop by or write, they were surprised.

It was around this time that Charles took a job at the Flintstones Theme Park, but he wasn't happy there—at one point he told a friend it was too difficult, and he'd rather be working at a turf farm. On May 26, Charles worked his last shift at Flintstones. According to the RCMP, the last confirmed sightings of Charles was later that same day, when he cashed his last paycheque at the Royal Bank in Orchard Park, and then when he was hitching a ride back into Kelowna. But a little more research on Denise's behalf suggested sightings considerably later than that. ❦

Searching for Answers

Some would call it serendipity that led Denise to book her stay at the Pandosy Inn. Denise would say it was common sense: she'd planned a lengthy visit, and the Pandosy Inn provided a kitchenette at a reasonable price. Still, it was a stroke of luck that, soon after her arrival, she noticed a campsite directly across the street: the Tiny Town Tent and Trailer Campground. And shortly after her arrival, she learned it was the same campground where Charles had eventually pitched his tent. By this time, Denise discovered that the campground, tucked away in a corner of Kelowna, was commonly thought to attract a rougher crowd. That's not to say everyone who stopped for the night was on the wild side. Families often used the site for a night or two while visiting or passing through the Okanagan. But its out-of-the-way location attracted the party crowd or young people looking for a good time. Denise was nervous to check it out and later said that it was a "very uncomfortable place to visit," but she was determined as well. Armed with photos of Charles, she crossed the street and made her way to the campground office.

"The first person I met there was Kevin Trent Egan," Denise said, adding she met him outside the campground office. "He was very uncomfortable with me, and said that I would have to speak to the manager when he got back." Denise thought it odd that Egan didn't talk about Charles when she introduced herself and explained her mission—in her short stay in the Okanagan she'd already come to the conclusion that her son seemed to have "met half of Kelowna in his time there and anyone who had met him had a lot to say about Charles." Egan could recall the chatty young man with the English accent, but he didn't have any stories about Charles to share. Denise didn't press him any further. Instead, she sat beside Egan, waiting in the hot and stifling July heat, until Phil Flett, Tiny Town's manager, returned. The interaction turned out to be even more distressing than she might have imagined.

"When Flett arrived back at Tiny Town, I approached him and asked if he remembered Charles," Denise said, adding that she showed Flett photographs of her son. "Flett acknowledged that he remembered Charles and that they had recently tidied up the shed and had thrown his belongings out." Then Flett walked over to the shed, grabbed the only remaining items that belonged to Charles—a small paper bible, a rosary and one of Charles' bootstraps—and handed them to Denise. For some inexplicable reason, family photographs and expensive-to-replace identification were tossed away while these seemingly insignificant items were spared from the garbage heap.

Clutching these small mementos of her son, Denise left the campground, her eyes swimming in tears, and her mind even more confused than before. The next day, May 12, 1990, other items belonging to Charles surfaced: one pink and one white short-sleeved, button-down collar shirt and a toiletry bag. And a week later, during Denise's stop in Vancouver, a grey-and-pink sweatshirt with "Max" written on it, and a white-and-navy cotton sweater with a sailboat on the front, were returned to her. For now, the three small items were all that remained of Charles and were the only physical evidence she could find that her son had ever been to Kelowna.

In a 1990, CHBC-TV interview, Flett called Charles "sharp," "clean cut" and "good looking" and described how, about two or three weeks after the weekend of May 26, 1989, the date police first believed Charles was last seen, Flett packed up Charles' tent and belongings and put them into storage. He then explained how the following spring, after no one had come to claim the items that included personal photographs and iden-tification, they were destroyed. In 1992, when asked during another CHBC-TV television interview what prompted him to make such an irrevocable decision, Flett called Charles a "tran-sient from Europe," and asked, "How would we know who to get a hold of?" When the interviewer pushed further, asking if Flett had heard any rumours about what might have happened to Charles, Flett maintained he had no idea. He hadn't heard a thing. ❧

CONFLICTING VIEWS

Joanne, however, tells a different story from Phil Flett when it comes to the last time she'd seen or spoken with Charles. She remembers Charles ringing her apartment buzzer one hot summer night, sometime in July—long after the May date police repeatedly referred to. Charles wanted to visit, but Joanne was hosting a dinner party at the time. Her brother, Peter, was visiting for the first time in five years, and it wasn't a good time for the boisterous Charles to pop by unannounced, so she declined. Joanne's dispute with the May 26 date continued because she remembered seeing Charles in August, this time at Kelowna's Live Wire Night Club, but she was with friends, and again, she didn't manage to chat with him directly.

After Joanne's information was passed on to the RCMP, they bent a little when it came to publicizing Charles' points last seen. They gave some credence to Joanne's story about speaking to Charles in July, partly because she actually spoke with him, and he identified himself, and because investigators could confirm her brother had his holidays in July. In a statement made to the RCMP in June 1992, Joanne's brother also affirmed that he heard the intercom conversation. These factors all supported Joanne's rendition of the events of that night in July. But police don't call her sighting of him at the nightclub a confirmed sighting because she admits she only saw him from a distance and hadn't spoken to him directly. In any case, after August 1989, there were no sightings of Charles.

Denise both welcomed and was disturbed by the news. It gave her and investigators more to work with in their search. But it also left Denise with the nagging question of why Charles hadn't called home. With what Denise knew of her son, and what his friends confirmed about Charles, his lack of contact with his family wasn't at all like him. Was it possible that Charles had gotten himself involved with something that was out of character for him—something that he knew his family wouldn't approve of? Now more than ever, Denise was convinced— something or someone had prevented Charles from connecting with his family. She was sure that if Charles was alive, he needed her help. If he was dead, she was going to find out what happened to her son. And why.

With a lot to think about, and feeling a mixed bag of emotions, Denise prepared to leave Kelowna. She knew she'd covered a lot of ground. But she still hadn't gotten what she came for—her son.

The trip home must have been depressing. Denise had no idea when she'd be able to afford another trip to Canada, but she had every intention of continuing her sleuthing long distance. As it turned out, it was another two long years before she set foot in the country of Charles' birth. ॐ

THE BODY TRIP

Until 1992, Denise's ongoing search took on the form of a long-distance investigation, but it was no less expensive. She maintained her newspaper advertisements. She culled through hundreds of family photos and designed a missing person's poster that showed Charles clean shaven and at his most familiar, and Charles with facial hair. Photographs of him in the context of different activities might jog a memory more than a simple mug shot would, so Denise included pictures of Charles as a shining young gentleman, all dressed up in a snazzy suit, and others where he was ready for the ski hill or just hanging out.

When she did embark on that second journey, she and her husband had to mortgage their home to help fund their costs. In a television interview, Stuart said that money could be replaced, but Charles could not. Still, with her son's plight always first and foremost in Denise's mind, tension in the relatively new marriage was mounting. Denise's health was suffering, and she wasn't eating properly. She found it difficult to focus on work and had to sell her beauty salon at a loss to help pay the mounting search costs. Everything in her life was snowballing out of control, and only one thing could stop the momentum—finding Charles.

Denise arrived in Canada on March 11, 1992, booked herself back into the Pandosy Inn and hit the ground running. She was alone this time but eager to start her search. Her plan was to spend four weeks following up on leads she'd uncovered since her visit in 1990 and to continue raising awareness about Charles' plight. By now she'd developed an intricate, colour-coded filing system separating leads from newspaper articles and personal contacts. She'd organized a working routine of securing missing person's posters to light posts and shop doors, slipping them into mailboxes, placing ads in newspapers and knocking on front doors.

This time her efforts paid off with several witnesses coming forward with information. One individual, who asked to remain anonymous, told Denise he thought he'd seen Charles on Sunday, May 14, 1989. It was Mother's Day. The witness claimed he saw an older, grey-haired gentleman who was the captain of a white and cream-coloured boat, accompanied by another rugged-looking fellow.

"They observed [them] picking up young men, two at a time, and going out onto Okanagan Lake," Denise said, adding the witness believed Charles was one of the young men who'd been picked up. "When the older, grey-haired man realized he was being observed, he circled around the lake until the witness had gone." The witness in question thought perhaps the older men were selling drugs to the young men and took note of the registration number on the boat and reported his suspicions to the police.

Later, another witness came forward saying that he, too, had seen Charles at Jonathan Seagulls, another Kelowna bar, and that Charles was in the company of an older, grey-haired man with "piercing blue eyes." This witness said he spoke with Charles, warned him about the gentleman he was with and suggested that the man was dangerous. It was never determined if the two grey-haired men that witnesses reportedly saw Charles with were one and the same individual, but at one point, police thought they'd tracked down someone who bore a strong resemblance to some of the witness descriptions. The only problem was that this fellow had died the year earlier. The only bit of hope police had of determining if the man in question knew Charles was to check if any information was on the man's personal computer. Sadly, that, too, led investigators to a dead end.

On March 16, another tip was delivered to Denise at the Pandosy Inn, this one in the form of an anonymous note:

> Dear Mrs Allan
> I seen your add in The paper looking for your Son
> I seen him in tiny tent Town May 26. We were Partying
> AnD two people knocked him out. But he Died. His
> Body is in the Lake By the Bridge.

It was earth-shattering information to receive, but Denise had to know if there was any truth to the claims. By now the RCMP might have been entertaining the possibility that Charles was dead, but they still weren't buying the story that he was a victim of foul play. However, if the media coverage over the last three years was any indication, the official RCMP stance on the case seemed to oscillate like a pendulum in search of a home. One moment they were suggesting Charles left of his own free will; the next they were considering he might have been a suicide. And then, of course, they seemed to work off and on with the theory that Charles was looking to get away from his family. But murder—even after three years had passed since Charles disappeared—was something the authorities continued to steer clear of even remotely considering. "We have no reason to suspect foul play. I know it's unusual. He's missing. He's been missing for three years, but there's no evidence at all to indicate that something serious happened to him," Kelowna Crime Stoppers spokesperson Dennis Schwartz told Adrienne Skinner from CHBC News in 1992. "We just don't know where he is."

The unsigned note didn't alter the police's stance a whole lot. Scouring the bottom of Okanagan Lake, which stretches 157 kilometres in length, three kilometres in width and reaches depths of 240 metres, was a momentous and extremely expensive suggestion. And according to the RCMP, there wasn't any need: no bodies were at the bottom of the lake. One officer told the media that over the years, several dives into its murky depths had taken place, particularly near the floating bridge that was suggested in the note. "If there was a body down there, it would have been discovered by now," the officer said.

In the years since that statement was made, the RCMP would find themselves eating their words several times over. In fact, on April 11, 1992, less than a month after Denise received the anonymous note, *The Daily Courier* reported that, "Records show 10 people went missing and are presumed drowned (in the lake) after boating or fishing accidents since 1972." But when Denise received that first note, investigators were still reluctant to start a search. If there was any investigating to do in the lake, it would have to begin with Denise.

Denise had to know if there was any truth to the new information she'd received in the note. She'd made her decision—she wasn't going to leave Kelowna until she found her son. She'd made enough friends in the city that by now she'd developed a network of people around her who cared about her plight, and by March 29, 1992, volunteer divers were making rounds along the bridge, moving their way from the shoreline to the lift span, searching out areas where in the past everything from stolen goods to dead bodies had been recovered. But day after day they came up empty, save a few odd bits of clothing and personal items. This was understandable, given that the lake's sandy bottom is in constant flux. A diver could spot something unusual, and then minutes later, whatever it was he'd seen would have disappeared. "If there is a body down there, the chance is 50-50 either way you could find it," diver Trish Dobson told *The Daily Courier* on April 3. "Okanagan Lake plays a lot of tricks. The body might be covered over with silt, but it might also be uncovered."

And the deeper you go, the darker the murky waters become. They needed a little help. Denise hired a submersible camera from International Sea Search out of Vancouver at the crippling cost of $1000 per day, but it took a few days before it could be shipped up from a job in Seattle. When the camera finally arrived, the company kindly donated their time to the search efforts, giving Denise more manpower to work with, but the cost of the camera rental would be frightening.

Shortly after divers started searching, Denise received a second note, this one picked up by a cab driver who had been instructed to drive to a telephone booth. Once there, the driver retrieved the note and delivered it to Denise at the Pandosy:

Mrs. Allan
Your Diving on The Wrong SiDe oF The BRiDge.

By the fourth day, the submersible camera was on site, combing the sandy bottom of Okanagan Lake while Denise searched for the man who delivered the second note to the cabbie, Craig Kosowan. Kosowan had told *The Daily Courier* that it wasn't unusual for a cabbie to pick up and deliver something for a client, but something was different about this scenario. Kosowan described the man handing him the note to be in his "mid-20s with medium-length blond hair, wearing a white T-shirt, cut-off jeans and sunglasses," and he was very nervous. After he gave Kosowan the message, the individual left the area on a white mountain bike. Denise was anxious to find the mysterious man. So were the police. His identity was never confirmed.

After the four long days of dawn-to-dusk searching, the RCMP decided to join in the effort. And then at 10:14 AM on Friday, April 3, on the sixth day of the search and at a depth of 40metres, volunteers from International Sea Search discovered what RCMP had previously argued wasn't there—the body of a man. The RCMP weren't on site at the time the discovery was made, so members of the International Sea Search called them in. The body was free and hadn't been restrained in any way, so police divers were able to bring the body to the surface by 12:15 PM. There was no skin on the face, hands and feet, but the parts of the body covered by clothing remained intact.

Denise also wasn't at the shoreline when the discovery was made, she'd been asked to keep her distance because she was told her presence was distracting some of the searchers. So she wasn't expecting to see two police officers screech up to the Pandosy Inn, as she explained it, true Starsky-and-Hutch fashion. Understandably, their news upset Denise. "I was in tears and went into the bathroom for some privacy, and cried," Denise remembers. She was distraught, yes—overwhelmed with exhaustion and overwrought with sadness. But by this point in her search, she'd expected this kind of end to her saga. She certainly wasn't falling apart or unable to think clearly. It wasn't as though Charles had been suddenly killed in a car accident and the shock was new and paralyzing.

Denise's memory of what happened next seems like something that came out of a made-for-TV movie, not real life. When she finally emerged from the bathroom, she discovered an ambulance had appeared, and she was being encouraged by the two police officers to go with the paramedics to the hospital for a check-up and rest. Denise agreed.

The RCMP would later go on record saying they'd taken Denise to the hospital because of their concern for her wellbeing. Denise remembers it differently. She said she was herded into the ambulance without any of her personal items. She called for her "Mum"—over the years Joyce Anderson and her husband Ray, managers at the Pandosy Inn, had become like parents to Denise, and Denise had taken to calling Joyce "Mum." Neither the ambulance attendants nor the officers appeared to understand her request, even when she asked specifically for Joyce. Either way, Denise found herself locked inside an ambulance with only an attendant by her side and her fears to keep her company.

A general practitioner supervised Denise during her hospital stay, which stretched from the originally suggested few hours to a few days. She endured the weekend in the hospital, not knowing if the body discovered was indeed that of her son or some other poor soul. Newspaper and media reports on the other hand, blared stories with such headlines as "Mom's nightmare over," "Body in lake ends Mum's agony," "Lake horror ends mum's tragic hunt" and the ridiculous "Mother rests as police examine body from lake."

Late that Sunday night, while still under a doctor's care, Denise was approached by the coroner who wanted to gather information for the death certificate he was filing on Charles. When Denise asked if they had made a positive identification of the body, the coroner said no, but they were certain it was

Charles. "I asked how he could complete a death certificate for a body you do not know to who it belongs," Denise said. She also argued that the description of the clothes worn by the man they'd discovered didn't sound like anything Charles would wear. But the coroner continued to probe for information on Charles' physique and identifying features. Denise remembers the coroner getting the information he needed to complete the death certificate and leaving some time around midnight, on April 5, 1992.

Completely wrung out and devastated, all Denise wanted to do was go home. She booked herself out of the hospital on Monday morning. "We waited all day, listening to the news, waiting and waiting for confirmation that it was Charles," she said. Stuart, in the meantime, had been making plans to arrive in Kelowna with a pathologist from England. If nobody else cared to make sure that the body her team had discovered was indeed Charles, Denise certainly did, especially since Denise had every intention of taking her son's remains home for burial.

But before the day was out, Denise would find herself on yet another emotional roller coaster and in a mad rush to get in touch with Stuart to change their plans. The coroner had handed her a press release dated April 6. After a forensic post-mortem examination, it was believed the body in the lake belonged to a man aged 50 or older. Furthermore, a dental comparison between the man in the lake and Charles' dental records were not a match.

Television and radio news shows were quick to retract their earlier claims. Now the headlines blazed "British mom continues search for missing son," "Search for Horvath goes on" and "Missing tourist still a mystery." By April 9, the remains discovered in the lake were identified as that of 64-year-old John Edgar Dickson of Kelowna. He was last seen on May 7, 1985, on Abbott Street, and his death was ruled a suicide.

The police also found themselves defending their, at best, spotty involvement in the case. Townsfolk were wondering why police seemed so disinterested in Charles' case from the very beginning. Charles' friends were vocal in their disapproval, going on record, saying that Denise, and not the police, had uncovered any leads in their friend's whereabouts. RCMP Inspector Dick Smith defended his team. "We are trying desperately to use our heads in this investigation and not our hearts...we can't be running off hither and yon." The RCMP were now saying they had assigned a senior officer with "a good track record in homicide investigations" to the case. Suddenly Charles had risen from the ranks of the merely missing to a homicide—at least for a time.

Denise also found herself with a lot of collateral damage to repair. When the body was first discovered, and everyone assumed it belonged to Charles, all the posters she'd diligently tacked up throughout town were torn down. Not only was she physically, mentally and emotionally exhausted, but she also faced the task of replacing all her posters if she wanted Charles' story to remain in the public eye.

Ironically, Denise would later discover that her ISS team was as hesitant as she was in thinking the body they'd recovered belonged to Charles. They thought the gentleman they recovered was larger than what fit Charles' description, and he was wearing what appeared to be odd clothing for a young man Charles' age. The RCMP, on the other hand, told Denise that the body recovered was clothed with corduroy pants, long johns, Hush Puppy shoes and a cardigan. "I said this clothing would be more what my grandfather would wear, not a young man," Denise remembered. Then again, she started wondering if perhaps his killers had redressed Charles. At this point, anything was possible.

Once again, Denise was left alone in her search. After being in Kelowna and the Lower Mainland for a full six weeks, Stuart arrived in Vancouver to meet Denise, and the couple stayed another week in Canada. Denise had one more errand on her agenda before she left for England. She had managed to track down a fellow who helped Charles put his tent up at Tiny Town. Denise had learned about Gordy Happ, one of Charles' acquaintances who was living in Vancouver at that time, and she had arranged to meet with him. Gordy, Stuart and Denise flew back to Kelowna to look through the list of campsite residents during Charles' stay there. Happ then identified Gino (Eugene) Bourdin as someone who knew Charles. It wasn't long before Denise tracked Gino down and learned a little more about her son's last known whereabouts.

"Gino told us about his friendship with Charles, and about the party and Charles' tent being taken down," Denise explained. Gino also remembered the party being on the Victoria Day long weekend. At the time, the speculation was that the May 26 date of the party, provided by the writer of the anonymous note, coincided with the Victoria Day long weekend, but Denise later discovered that wasn't true. The May long weekend always falls on the weekend on or before May 24, Queen Victoria's birthday, and in 1989, it landed on the weekend of the 19th. So the party, which no one seemed to have been aware of— despite its size and the apparent presence of 75 bikers on their way to the Falklands Stampede—took place on the 19th and not the 26th. Had the letter writer mixed up the dates? They had definitive proof that Charles was alive on the 26th, so was it possible that he had been involved in an altercation on that party weekend but didn't die? Or were the notes about Charles a hoax, after all?

Not to be deterred, Denise looked at the new but conflicting information as answers to previously unanswered—and unasked—questions. Gino also told them about photographs that were taken during the party. Getting her hands on those photos before leaving Canada was a priority, especially now.

It took a lot of money to develop the pictures and identify the people in the photos, which, for the most part, held images of bikers and their bikes, people partying and the campground itself. Only one photo had a face in the background that might have been Denise's son. "At least I was able to see Charles' tent," she said.

Still, because the police had initially dated Charles as missing since May 26, 1989, the photos of the party from the weekend earlier were really irrelevant to the investigation.

At this point in Denise's search, she knew she was piecing together her son's life in the spring of 1989 bit by miniscule bit. It was clearly a step or two forward, and a step or two back in many instances. But she was convinced she was making progress. She believed that although the note writer who led her to spending thousands of dollars in an underwater search—only a portion of which was recouped from the RCMP—may have potentially given her misleading information, there was a grain of truth in some of what he had to say. At least she had something to work on when she returned to England.

A PUSH FOR PUBLICITY

Just two short weeks after arriving home, Denise was once again on a plane and flying to North America. After trading in her tickets for a business trip she had planned to accompany Stuart on, Denise was bound for Los Angeles to talk to Cosgrove

Muerer and the producers of *Unsolved Mysteries* to lobby them to do a show on her son's story. From there she flew to Toronto, to visit old friends and to thank the producers of *Missing Treasures* for their production.

Although she didn't visit Kelowna again during that trip, a promise her husband Stuart elicited from her, she kept in contact with the media there. *The Daily Courier* ran a story outlining how Hollywood was getting involved in the local story. Stories also ran in the *Evening Courier* in Denise's hometown of Halifax, England, and in *Woman* magazine. Denise may have had to leave Kelowna, but she by no means stopped working on her son's case.

Some time after April 3, 1992, and what Denise came to call her "body trip," police telephoned some of Charles' father's relations in Canada to see what they could find out about the young man. Denise later learned of what she called "poison telephone conversations" between the police and her ex in-laws. Some past hurts hadn't obviously healed, and some of her ex-husband's relatives had a less than favourable opinion of the woman who they believed jilted their Max.

Although the information may have jaded the RCMP's opinion of Denise and Charles' relationship and delayed their work on the case, it did a lot more immediate damage to Denise's efforts. When her attempts to have her son's story aired on *Unsolved Mysteries* were made public, officials from the show received information about the content of these telephone calls.

If the comments were true—that Charles had really orches-trated his own disappearance in order to get away from his mother—it brought the entire story into question. Denise was devastated and angry. There was no telling how much damage the malicious rumours could do to the case—if indeed anyone thought there was a case any longer. Denise's frustration was further fuelled by the fact that it appeared to her that nobody showed any interest in contacting any of Charles' relatives in the UK, nor had they tried to talk to any of his former teachers or friends to ask their opinions on Charles' relationship with his mother. The information received by *Unsolved Mysteries* was uncorroborated before it was sent to them.

Unsolved Mysteries cancelled the scheduled filming of "Canadian Camper," their story on Charles. Denise, who had arrived in Canada in November 1992 especially for the filming, had been making her way across the country, again retracing Charles' earlier journey and hanging posters. Her health was fragile, and a case of shingles erupted on her skin before she arrived in Vancouver, a few days before her scheduled interviews with *Unsolved Mysteries*. That's when she received a call from David Massar, the segment director, telling her that production on the segment had been cancelled because the producers believed the information they'd received was true, and that Charles was nothing more than a runaway.

At this point, Denise didn't know if she had it in her to continue. After a journey across Canada, during gruelling winter conditions, and coping with her health issues, Denise was on her way to speak with Massar in his home in Nelson. Massar sat with Denise at her motel room, culling through photographs and hearing her stories about the baby Charles, Charles as a little boy, Charles the young man in the French Foreign Legion, Charles the son who made Denise's life worth living. Denise recalled Massar's obvious emotion over her story, and how he promised to do everything he could to push the producers to go ahead with the filming.

Denise had made huge strides in correcting some misconceptions, but she still had to travel to Kelowna to explain to the media there why filming was cancelled. The activity surrounding the case and Denise's November 1992 visit once again generated information, along with a push from an anonymous young woman who'd stopped by the Pandosy Inn with a message for Denise to end her search. She'd never find him, the tipster said. Denise, who wasn't in at the time, anxiously awaited the return of the young woman. But she never came back: no one was surprised since the woman had said she was too afraid to give any more details.

Denise wasn't about to let the woman's warning stop her when nothing else had. In August 1993, a crew of 17 turned up in Kelowna and spent four days filming the rest of "Canadian Camper." *Missing Treasures* aired their segment on July 4, 1992, and on October 24 of the same year. And Crime Stoppers has aired Charles' mystery several times over the years. If Charles is out there, somewhere, in need of help or medical assistance, Denise stands firm in her desire to rally round him. If he's dead, as the RCMP now believes is the case, then he needs burying. ∾

TIME GOES BY, SLOWLY

It's been 20 years since Charles Horvath last spoke to his mother. Twenty years since there were any confirmed sightings of the young man. Over those years, Denise continued to travel back and forth to Canada, spreading the word about her son and pushing for more and more tips. She's endured unkind hoaxes and false hopes. At one point, someone was convinced they'd seen Charles and that he was married and had a child. Denise tracked down the person in question. He looked a lot like Charles. But he wasn't Charles.

Another time, folks were convinced Charles was back in Kelowna. The man in question was honked at while stopped at a red light, and the driver of the car beside him told him to call his mother. Again, the sightings were proven to be of a Charles look-alike.

Over the years, Denise has lived through at least three more bodies being pulled from the depths of Okanagan Lake and the discovery of a human skull and bones on Kelowna's Westside. None of the bodies pulled from the lake were Charles, and the human bones have yet to be identified. But each time such a discovery is made, Denise goes through an unimaginable array of emotions wondering if this time they've found Charles—if this time she can bring her son's body home to rest.

Whenever possible, Denise visits Kelowna in May, throws 20 white roses—one for every year she shared with Charles—onto the lake that some believe holds the key to his fate, meets with the media and updates missing persons posters. And she still has a message Charles left on her answering machine sometime after embarking on his cross-Canada excursion: "Mom, it's me, Charles. I'm at Gabby's. Will you call me? Please." She has listened to it so often it's embedded in her memory…but it does her soul good to keep the recording.

On January 8, 2006, Charles' beloved Nana passed away. Before she died, she wrote a plea for her grandson, saying how she feared during their last farewell that they'd never see each other again. "Another Christmas has come and gone without our family knowing the fate of my only grandson, Charles. Soon I shall be 80 years old. If you know who took Charles from our lives or if you know where his body is located, please find the courage to come forward…"

Denise is still trying to find the answer to that plea, and although she accepts that Charles may have gotten involved with some unsavoury people and done some things he would have known his mother wouldn't approve of, she repeatedly says she won't give up her search until she finds Charles, or dies looking. He is her son, after all, regardless what he might have gotten himself into.

In December 2004, RCMP Corporal Lisa Cullen took over the file. Although it doesn't command the priority of new cases, she reviews it whenever she has a spare moment. A mother herself, Cullen is touched by Denise's plight. In May 2008, the media interviewed the officer for a special newscast. Cullen challenged people to come forward with information, reminded viewers that a lot had changed in 19 years, assured them not to be afraid—like the woman who, years earlier, had managed to coax herself to the Pandosy Inn to speak with Denise but ran away in terror before she managed to talk to her.

"I don't think we can judge those people that aren't coming forward, because we don't know why they're not coming forward. Obviously they have good reasons," Cullen told reporters, adding that every time Denise returns to Kelowna, new tips are generated. Unfortunately, a lot of those tips are secondary, and Cullen urged people to keep calling in with tips. "Somebody knows. Somebody absolutely knows what happened to him."

It's what the people who knew Charles in Kelowna have been saying all along. And were he alive today, and with the publicity Denise has managed to maintain about her son's case, someone would have come forward with information on how to get in touch with him. He wasn't the kind of guy who liked to go through life anonymously.

"Charles wanted attention all the time," Joanne once said. "He simply did not want to be alone [and] I think for him to disappear himself he would have to be terribly alone. That is not like him…Somewhere out there someone knows something."

And someday, that someone will come forward.

Chapter Seven

The King of Hearts—Tanya Van Cuylenborg and Jay Roland Cook

Young love. High school sweethearts. Who can forget the euphoria? Everything is sunshine and blue skies, birds singing and nary a care in the world. That's the way it was for 18-year-old Tanya Van Cuylenborg and her 20-year-old boyfriend, Jay Roland Cook. The couple was over the moon in love. And better still, it was a relationship both of their parents supported. So much so that when Jay's father Gordon asked his son to do an overnight errand for him, he thought nothing of young Tanya tagging along. It was almost a given. They seemed so right for each other, and in the six months since they'd started dating, their families noticed that they were rarely apart. If they weren't working or at school, chances were that wherever you saw one, you'd find the other.

Gordon's errand required Jay and Tanya to travel from the Vancouver Island community of Oak Bay to Seattle, Washington, to pick up some furnace parts. The couple was excited.

It would mean an overnight excursion that amounted to a mini-holiday in their young world—a first for the ardent couple. And on Wednesday, November 18, 1987, Jay and Tanya hopped into Gordon's tan-coloured 1977 Ford van and started out for their big adventure equipped with a tank of gas, enough money to see them to their destination and back, and $570 in cash and travellers' cheques to use for the purchase of the furnace parts.

Starting out along Oak Bay's knotted and gnarled roadways, lined with the Garry oak that is the Bay's namesake, Tanya and Jay made their way to downtown Victoria and boarded the auto ferry service to Port Angeles, Washington. Along with the scenic hour-and-a-half journey through the Strait of Juan de Fuca, the couple planned to drive along Route 101 and then Route 3 to take in the views from the port to Shelton and then Bremerton. That's where they'd catch another ferry to Seattle, pick up the furnace parts the following day, and then make their way back home. It was the perfectly planned overnighter—or at least it started out that way.

No one ever knew anything had gone awry until the couple didn't show up at home when they were expected on November 19. Red flags rose almost immediately: the kids were reliable and would have called if they were held up somewhere. William Van Cuylenborg told *Unsolved Mysteries* that it was completely out of character for his daughter not to call if she expected to be late. "When Tanya did not phone the next evening when they were supposed to be returning, my wife became apprehensive. So I tried to downplay it for my wife's sake and probably to reassure myself that everything would be okay." When neither set of parents had heard anything from either of the young people by the morning of November 20, everyone knew something was very wrong. The police were called in. ∾

RETRACING THEIR STEPS

At first, following Jay and Tanya's trail was fairly straightforward. It was easy to confirm that the couple had boarded the ferry in Victoria. And because police inquiries led them to the village of Allyn, they could surmise the youngsters had managed to take in part of their planned sightseeing. Allyn is a seaside community overlooking Puget Sound's North Bay and Case Inlet, and it stands in the shadows of Mount Rainier and the North Cascades on the mainland. The couple bought something at a roadside stop in Allyn and shortly afterwards purchased their ferry ticket for Bremerton to Seattle.

That's where the police met with a dead end: they couldn't find a witness to place Jay and Tanya, or the Ford that the couple had been driving, on the ferry that night or any time thereafter. And it was increasingly evident that they hadn't overnighted outside the newly built Kingdome Stadium as planned. It was as if they'd simply vanished, without the fanfare that often accompanies acts of violence.

Hours turned into days as the searchers continued combing the countryside and waterways surrounding Bremerton and throughout the Snohomish and Skagit counties. And then on Tuesday, November 24, a leisurely stroll along the outskirts of the tiny Skagit County community of Alger led one man to a gruesome discovery. There, amid the thick underbrush in a ditch lining Parsons Creek Road lay the body of a young woman. It wasn't long before she was identified as Tanya Van Cuylenborg. Her parents were devastated—nothing could be worse. As it happens, their nightmare was only beginning at that point. Soon they'd learn their lively and vivacious daughter, who was young, in love and had her whole life to look forward to, had died from a gunshot wound to the back of her head, but not before being brutally raped.

The search now heated up for Jay and the Cooks' van. With statistics from think tanks such as the Violence Policy Centre suggesting that as many as 92 percent of female homicide victims are killed by someone they knew, there was a time in the initial stages of the investigation where things weren't looking so good for Tanya's boyfriend. Until Jay was discovered, he could also conceivably be considered a person of interest in Tanya's death. The Cooks didn't know what to think, nor did the Van Cuylenborgs. Jay's mother told *Unsolved Mysteries* that "…because they hadn't found Jay…it looked like Jay might even be a suspect. [The police] told us to be prepared for that."

On the other hand, police were equally concerned for Jay's safety. Fairly early into the investigation, it became clear that the more likely scenario was that Jay was also in danger. Things didn't get any better when the Ford van was discovered near a Greyhound Bus Depot parking lot in downtown Bellingham, Whatcom County, on Wednesday, November 25. So far, the trail led investigators across three Washington counties, a considerable area to search for clues, as well as the missing 20-year-old. ∾

A SECOND BODY

And then the day of truth arrived. Thanksgiving Day, November 26, 1987—only two days after the discovery of Tanya's body, though for everyone involved it must have felt like a lifetime. This time it was hunters who found a dead body.

According to Stephen G. Michaud and Hugh Aynesworth, who penned a story about the case in the 1991 book *Murderers Among Us*, Jay's body was recovered under High Bridge "near the town of Monroe, in Snohomish County, 20 miles or so northwest of Seattle, and roughly 45 miles south of Alger in Skagit County."

He'd been brutally beaten and strangled to death, and whoever killed him used some type of ligature, perhaps a cord or wire, to commit the deed. A cursory examination led investigators to believe the body was that of Jay Cook, but the Snohomish

County Medical Examiner awaited the receipt of dental records before making it official.

On Monday, November 30, the *Skagit Valley Herald* gave readers the much-expected news: the missing young Canadian was certainly no murderer; he was a victim.

At this point, police had found two murder victims and a recovered stolen van. During a detailed search of the area surrounding the site where Jay's body was discovered, a trail led police to several pieces of evidence a couple of blocks away: Tanya's driver's licence, surgical gloves and a box of ammunition, as well as plastic ties similar to the ones they'd uncovered near Tanya's body—ties that could have been used to secure her in the van.

But it was all too convenient—it was as if the evidence was contrived, as if the only clues uncovered throughout the investigation were clearly staged for detectives to find. Detective Robert Gebo of the Seattle Police Department reinforced this idea when they spoke with reporters from *Unsolved Mysteries*. It was "…a sign to the police that you needn't look for fingerprints because I wore these gloves. And he [the perpetrator] has confidence that there's nothing that's going to connect him with these crimes." It appeared that the killer's confidence was well founded. Searches around the area where Tanya's body was discovered came up empty.

Although police were making some progress, it only led officers to more and more questions. What had happened here?

For a while police appeared to be favouring the theory that robbery was the motive for the attacks. The couple wasn't carrying an exorbitant amount of money, though the $570 could be a temptation for the right criminal. And because the couple was travelling in a van, it gave the killer or killers a means with which to carry out the crime. But there were other possibilities.

A ferry ticket was also discovered in the van, and both bodies were discovered on the mainland, considerably north of Seattle, so it was obvious that despite the absence of witnesses, it was most likely that Jay and Tanya did indeed board the ferry and were likely alive at that point. Police then reasoned it was possible that Tanya was the temptation for the attack—someone on the ferry, perhaps, might have spotted the couple and became enamoured with the young woman. Small talk could have led to a request for a ride, and the young people, not altogether worldly wise and thinking there couldn't be any harm in the request, may have agreed.

The ease with which the killer managed to connect with the young couple and exit the ferry with them without raising suspicion suggested to Detective Robert Gebo that the killer was an experienced and successful criminal—someone who could potentially re-offend if he wasn't apprehended and incarcerated.

Another telling detail that police uncovered during their search was what in effect made up a "murder kit" of sorts: plastic restraints, rubber gloves and ammunition. Because the items hadn't belonged to the victims, and they weren't something a person would normally carry, it seemed logical to theorize that the perpetrator had used each of these items before, maybe even carried these tools of his trade around with him.

Therefore, to some extent, it was a fair assumption that an attack had been planned that night. Sadly, Jay and Tanya happened to be at the wrong place at the wrong time, and their presence there earned themselves the lead roles as victims.

Police concluded that Tanya and Jay were both likely murdered on the night of November 18. The van would have disembarked at Seattle and was discovered at the farthest point north, evidence that suggested that Jay was killed first, his body dumped in a fairly remote area about 32 kilometres northwest of the Emerald City.

The ease with which the killer or killers manoeuvered throughout the state, often using county back roads and clearly avoiding any kind of detection, also suggests he knew the area. Leaving the van so far north could have been an attempt by the murderer or murderers to suggest that they had left the country via the I-5 and had entered Canada through Highway 99, when instead they had remained in the U.S. Then again, perhaps that's exactly what they did. ∾

ONE KILLER OR TWO?

The two methods of murder—gunshot and strangulation—also had investigators thinking that two different personalities were involved in the crime. The hands-on method of ligature strangulation suggested that Jay's murder was a more "intimate" act compared to the cold-blooded and detached shooting of Tanya.

One hole in the theory of two perpetrators was that it didn't seem likely that Jay and Tanya would have been willing to give two strangers a ride that night, unless, of course, they weren't aware of the second person until it was too late.

Another component of this crime suggested the involvement of a second person, even in a cursory way. While the rest of the world geared up for the season of peace and goodwill, the Cooks and Van Cuylenborgs were still deep in grief. And just when they may have thought they were starting to cope with their new reality, which meant a life without their children, both families received a series of greeting cards that started off with a personal salutation, the phrase "HALLELUHAH BLOODY JESUS," an incredibly distinctive writing style and details of their children's murders.

The author of the cards claimed to be the murderer, and the cards were mailed from three major cities: New York, Los Angeles and Seattle. But when investigators compared the DNA on the envelope to the DNA uncovered from Jay and Tanya, no match was made. Could the writer have been a witness or even an accomplice in the crimes? Or maybe the person was simply someone the murderer confided in? The cards came, unbidden and unwelcome, during at least three different holiday seasons, and then they stopped.

Police in Skagit and Snohomish counties, as well as law enforcement from Vancouver Island, spent countless hours examining and re-examining the evidence and comparing their findings to other unsolved cases in Washington State. The senseless deaths of these two young people haunted everyone involved in the investigation. "I don't see any reason to kill these kids," former homicide detective Rick Bart told *Daily Herald* reporter Diana Hefley in December 2008, more than 20 years after the deadly outing that cost two youths their lives. "I don't understand why they're dead. It made no sense at all."

The murders, closely followed by the media, also haunted the residents of Washington, a state that's sadly all too familiar with violent deaths associated with history-making serial murderers such as Ted Bundy and the Green River Killer. Did Tanya and Jay fall victim to a serial killer—a predator responsible for one of several unsolved killing sprees? Perhaps the individual is someone connected to one of several cold cases in the state. Maybe he's in prison for another crime?

Or maybe he's dead.

Among the possibilities investigators toyed with was trying to compare the murders of Tanya and Jay to several other unsolved cases that were thought to be linked to Charles

T. Sinclair, also known as the "Coin Shop Killer." In the decade spanning 1980 to 1990, more than a dozen police departments were tracking Sinclair at different times, suspecting him in a string of upheavals that included murder, robbery and rape, and extended from Vancouver, BC, to Vacaville, California; Kansas City, Missouri; Watertown, New York; Billings, Montana; and Spokane, Washington.

He was dubbed the Coin Shop Killer because many of his victims were owners of coin shops who police suspected agreed to meet with Sinclair at off hours for one reason or another, killing the storeowner before robbing him of his wares. But there were exceptions to Sinclair's routine—it was one of the reasons why FBI behavioural specialists and other criminal profilers struggled with the decision to label Sinclair a serial killer.

In a previous life, Sinclair was a well-respected Navy veteran who'd served in the Vietnam War and worked in the oilfield and in a farmer's field before opening his own gun shop. He was married, had two teenagers and, for all intents and purposes, was living the American dream. But running a business costs money, and Jefferson County police officer Pete Piccini, who'd spent a good portion of his career tracking Sinclair's movements, told *Seattle Post-Intelligencer* reporter Mike Barber that the first crime he suspected Sinclair of committing was a bank embezzlement of $30,000 in New Mexico. Sinclair and his family "went into the wind" under assumed names after the money went missing, resurfacing in Deming, Washington, which is in Whatcom County.

Sinclair's behaviour continued to devolve from there, but the one crime Sinclair was suspected of committing that bore a striking resemblance to the murder of Jay and Tanya was the mysterious disappearance of 64-year-old Robert D. Linton and his 62-year-old wife, Dagmar.

The couple from Stockton, California, had been making their way through Washington's Jefferson County to Expo '86 in Vancouver, BC, when they decided to set up their trailer in a Brinnon-area campground to take a day trip. They were never heard from again, nor were their bodies ever discovered. But their credit card was used several times, and at one point, yet another coin shop owner described the credit card user as being "taller than 6 feet 4 inches, big hair in a bandanna." It sounded like Sinclair to Piccini. Police were narrowing in on their suspect, but once the media caught wind of the story, Sinclair must have panicked, and his trail went cold. ∾

SIMILARITIES?

Like the Lintons, Jay and Tanya had passed through Brinnon during their ride along Route 101, and like the Lintons, the young couple was planning to take the ferry from Bremerton to Seattle. Vehicles belonging to both couples were discovered abandoned: the Lintons' truck at the Sea-Tac airport and Jay and Tanya's van in Bellingham. The similarities bore looking into. But if investigators were hoping for anything conclusive, such as a confession, it was not to be.

Sinclair was arrested on August 13, 1990, in Alaska. He was still using his pseudonym, Jimmy Charles Weir, and had been trying to purchase a farm when he was apprehended and placed in a Cook Inlet jail.

And while the wheels of justice were grinding and decisions were being made as to which state Sinclair would face trial in, law enforcement officials made the trip to Alaska to interrogate Sinclair for the crimes committed in their respective states. "He was cold as a snake on a stone," Piccini remembered. On October 30, 1990, while still in jail in Alaska, Sinclair died of a heart attack, taking his secrets with him. He was 44. But he left behind a storage locker full of mementoes from several of the crimes he was suspected of committing. It's not known if anything belonging to Jay and Tanya was discovered on the premises.

Early in the investigation of Jay and Tanya's murder, a $100,000 reward was established for information leading to the arrest of the responsible parties. In 2008, another effort was made to encourage the public to supply information through the promise of money. The Snohomish County sheriff's office also planned an initiative that originated in Florida when police tweaked an idea the U.S. army had used in Iraq.

In an effort to help troops remember the faces of war criminals, the army issued decks of playing cards, with each card displaying the photo of a different war criminal. Florida investigators took that concept and created a deck of cards that had a photo and information on a cold case on each card.

The initiative seemed like a good one to Snohomish County officials, and their personalized decks of 52 cold-case cards, complete with a toll-free telephone number to report information and the promise of a monetary award of up to $1000 if the information panned out, were distributed to inmates in Washington prisons in the fall of 2008.

Jay and Tanya's story is told on the King of Hearts.

Chapter Eight

Just Doing Their Jobs—
Lindsay Buziak and MaryAnn Plett

It was early February 2008, and it already looked like this was going to be a stellar year for Lindsay Buziak. The petite 24-year-old with a giant personality was one of the youngest of the roughly 1300 real estate agents working in the Victoria area of Vancouver Island, and she'd just received a dream call from a potential client. The woman on the phone had a foreign accent and was eager to purchase a million-dollar home before the day was out. In particular, the caller was interested in an empty house at 1702 DeSousa Place. Lindsay agreed to meet the woman at the location around 5:30 PM. It was Saturday, February 2.

A million-dollar house sale is a coup for any real estate agent. If Buziak's sale went through, it could fetch $34,000 in commissions for Re-Max Camosun, the Victoria-based company she worked for. Even though she wasn't the property's listing agent, Buziak could conceivably earn a quarter of that profit. She was excited at the prospect no doubt, but she was a little leery, too. Why hadn't the caller asked for Laurie Lidstone or Nancy DiCastri, the listing agents for the house? Why did the woman want her in particular to show the property? And why was the female caller so insistent about buying a house that day? It all seemed too good to be true.

Lindsay was young, but she wasn't foolish. She'd acquired her real estate licence soon after graduating from high school and had worked in the industry ever since. She was experienced enough to know that this call was out of the ordinary, and she shared her concerns with her co-workers.

Later in the day, the already strange situation got stranger. A man phoned, told Lindsay that his wife couldn't make the 5:30 PM appointment and that he'd meet her instead. The situation worried Lindsay enough that she talked about it with at least one of her friends, shared her concerns with her colleagues and called her boyfriend, Jason Zailo. Also an agent with the same company, Zailo agreed to check on Lindsay at some point during the appointment. The arrangement must have satisfied Lindsay sufficiently, because she prepared for her meeting and left the office.

Shortly after 6:00 PM, a man called 911 and asked the dispatcher to send police to check on the well-being of someone at 1702 DeSousa Place. While police were on their way, thinking they were attending to a routine call, emergency dispatchers received another 911 call. The call had come from inside the house, and the caller told police he'd found Lindsay Buziak. She was dead.

CHAOS REIGNS

At first, no one in the surrounding area really knew what was going on at the upscale property. But for an uninhabited cul-de-sac with houses still in various stages of construction, there was suddenly a lot of activity in the neighbourhood. The brand-new, five-bedroom, four-bathroom house in a subdivision that was under development was surrounded by yellow crime tape and officially declared a crime scene. The street was barricaded, and no one was allowed into the area. For the next 48 hours, forensic experts garbed from head to toe in white jumpsuits went over every inch of the house. Investigators and search-and-rescue crews combed through the yard, garages and other buildings in the cul-de-sac looking for anything that might prove to be evidence in the case. By the time the newspapers hit city streets that Monday, family and friends of Lindsay Buziak knew of her death, and police were calling it a homicide.

Still, the details were sketchy. Police declined to elaborate on the cause of death, but just knowing that someone had murdered the young woman was enough to throw the entire city into shock. No one who knew Lindsay could even remotely suggest a reason for the murder. "I don't think she's ever done anyone wrong," Gary Reitmayer told *Times Colonist* reporters. Reitmayer was Lindsay's uncle and a retired RCMP officer. "We have no idea what happened. It's a mystery to all of us. She was a kind-hearted, beautiful person." And yet, as the evidence was uncovered, and the public learned about the series of events that led Lindsay to 1702 DeSousa Place, it appeared the attack was anything but random.

"She was targeted, absolutely; it was a scheduled showing," Chris Markham, president-elect of the Victoria Real Estate Board told *Globe and Mail* reporters. Laurie Lidstone, one of the property's listing agents, agreed: "Someone specifically called this girl to show a vacant house. It sounds preplanned. It sounds premeditated."

It was up to the police to unravel the mystery and discover if there was any merit to what people were thinking.

Although police originally didn't divulge the identity of the 911-caller who had alerted them to the situation at DeSousa Place, it was later confirmed that Jason Zailo, who went to check on Lindsay as promised, had called the police. He was also the first person to discover Lindsay's body. On Wednesday, February 6, Jason was asked to return to the scene and walk investigators through the series of events as they occurred when he found the body. Police later conducted a search of the condo Lindsay and Jason shared, hoping to gain information on what might have attributed to the horrible crime, but they came up empty-handed. The public eventually learned that Buziak was found "stabbed to death against a wall in an upstairs bedroom."

What the police wouldn't elaborate on, even a year after the murder, were any theories they had as to motive. Was Lindsay's murder meant as a threat to someone else? Was she just in

the wrong place at the wrong time? Or was this horrible nightmare solely the makings of a deranged mind?

On Saturday, February 9, as many as 800 mourners
spilled onto View Street outside Victoria's St. Andrew's Cathe-
dral to pay their respects to Lindsay and to show their support for
her grieving family. Jeff Buziak, Lindsay's father, urged anyone
with information on his daughter's death to come forward.

And then all went silent. Saanich police told the media
that there'd be no additional updates. They also asked the family to refrain from talking to the media. In the real estate world,
and for Lindsay's family and friends, the murder hung in the air
like a dark cloud. But after a few months, things settled down.
"It was all the buzz for the first six months, and we were just
commenting the other day we don't hear a thing anymore,"
Lidstone told *Times Columnist* reporters on the anniversary of
Lindsay's murder.

Near the first-year anniversary of Lindsay's death, Saanich police broke their silence, giving the media an update on the
case in January 2009. They told the media that they'd conducted almost 1500 interviews. They'd also executed 30 search
warrants and investigated almost 800 tips. Some criticized the
police, saying they weren't doing enough to solve Lindsay's murder. The rumour mill churned with stories that this case was
"connected to a more important case," and investigators were
being stalled in their progress because of it.

Any criticism about how the police were handling the case was deflected by Reitmayer who told the *Vancouver Sun* that, "In order for something like this to get resolved, it requires a whole bunch of different pieces to come into place. We have to be somewhat patient."

Although there are never any guarantees in life, Lindsay's family still believes someone with information will come forward. "I believe there are people in this community who either know what went on, or parts of what went on," Jeff Buziak told reporters from the *Times Colonist*. The family still has high hopes that justice will be served.

In 1971, that's exactly what Jake Plett was thinking. ❧

BREAKING GROUND

In the 1970s, MaryAnn Plett was making a name for herself in a man's world. Real estate was still a male-dominated profession, but the young wife and mother of two sons was focused. She was a committed Christian who tried to live her faith in every aspect of her life, even when it came to deciding on her career choice. One day, shortly after she and her family moved into a new home in Edmonton in May 1968, MaryAnn felt called to check out the real estate options in the want ads. Within days she landed herself a job in the competitive world of buying and selling property. She was so successful in her newfound, God-directed career that her husband Jake was able to pursue his dream of returning to university.

For three years, high-energy, 29-year-old MaryAnn juggled motherhood with her job at Graham Realty, repeatedly won accolades for her sales performance and was generally well respected in her chosen profession. She was punctual, reliable, organized and communicated well with her colleagues. And she always let Jake know where she was and what she was doing. These qualities are what made her successful, so when she didn't call work or home on September 15, 1971, both her workmates and her husband were concerned.

Jake was the first to worry. He had only one class that day and was home by 11:00 AM. After calling Lyndon's babysitter to let her know she could send his five-year-old son home, Jake called MaryAnn's office, but she wasn't in. Jake knew MaryAnn was trying to sell a property near Looma, Alberta—she'd prayed about it during their morning prayers. Grant and Joyce Nelson, the owners of the Looma property, had recently purchased their dream home in Edmonton and were being stretched financially. They were also struggling with health issues and desperately needed relief from the worry the acreage in Looma represented. It was a problem that weighed heavily on MaryAnn; she'd sold the couple their new home and was determined to relieve them of the stress of two mortgages.

The secretary at MaryAnn's office told Jake that James Cooper had called again. MaryAnn had already shown him the property twice before, once on August 23 and again on September 9, and Cooper was calling to say he wanted to see it one more time before putting in an offer. It would be an answer to her prayer if Cooper actually bought the property, and MaryAnn was hoping he'd finally make a decision about it.

On the other hand, MaryAnn did have reservations about the man.

The mysterious Mr. Cooper was more than just a little odd. The usually gracious MaryAnn was somewhat disturbed by Cooper's behaviour. The man refused to meet at her office. Instead, he asked to be picked up at Bonnie Doon Shopping Centre. Retired Edmonton police detective Al Gowler told Wilfred Golbeck, freelancer to the *Edmonton Journal* in 1992, that Cooper would "appear out of nowhere at her car."

In his book *Valley of Shadows*, Jake said that MaryAnn told him and her co-workers that Cooper made her feel uncomfortable, and she had mentioned to her boss that she was "concerned about being out there alone with him." MaryAnn said that Cooper had a habit of mumbling and arguing with himself during their rides to the rural property, which MaryAnn had advertised as "just 19 miles from Bonnie Doon." It also seemed as though Cooper didn't consider punctuality a virtue, or he was simply inconsiderate, because for both of their first two meetings, he had kept MaryAnn waiting for quite some time.

Her lack of knowledge about the man likely added to MaryAnn's feeling of unease. The curt, stocky, middle-aged man with the "gruff voice" told MaryAnn that he was a businessman based in Winnipeg, Manitoba, and that he worked for a large American company. He also explained that he travelled frequently to the Edmonton area and was looking for an acreage to "store heavy equipment." However, he never gave MaryAnn his contact information, and she never saw him with a vehicle. This lack of information meant her colleagues didn't have any idea how to get in touch with the mystery man.

When MaryAnn didn't return to the office by the end of the day, her manager, Norm Schultz, called the Plett home. On hearing that MaryAnn hadn't been in touch with her office all day, Jake's initial worry multiplied exponentially. He phoned the property owners to see when they'd last spoken to MaryAnn. Jake was shocked to learn that the last time the couple had spoken with MaryAnn was the day earlier—they hadn't heard from her at all that day. More concerned than ever, Jake called for a babysitter, arranged to meet Schultz at the office, and the two men drove to the Looma-area property.

After scanning the acreage and failing to find any trace of MaryAnn, the Pletts' car or Mr. Cooper, Jake started canvassing the neighbours, asking if anyone noticed any action at the property or if they had seen a two-tone green Pontiac driving by. Schultz, in the meantime, called the office and arranged for MaryAnn's worried co-workers to meet him and Jake in Looma for a wider search of the area. The searchers arrived, accompanied by a car from the Sherwood Park Fire Department, and utilizing its searchlights, scoured what they could of the acreage. Calling her name over a loudspeaker, the group collectively held its breath, hoping for a reply. The group then split into teams and each car took a different route back to the city, hoping to cover as much ground between the property and the office as possible and stopping to question every gas station attendant along the way. It was a good plan but didn't yield a single clue as to the whereabouts of MaryAnn or her car.

As a dejected Jake prepared to leave the group, which by now had reconvened at Graham Realty's southside office on Whyte Avenue, he noticed his car driving by with a strange man in the driver's seat. It seemed to slow down as it passed by the office; Jake didn't notice if the car was slowing down for a red light or if the man inside was checking to see if there was any activity at the office. Either way, Jake grabbed one of MaryAnn's co-workers and rushed outside to follow the man. Unfortunately, by the time they got into a car of their own, the Pontiac was nowhere to be seen.

By this point, the usually calm Jake was anxious to talk to the police, who'd agreed to meet him at the family's home. The previous night, Jake and MaryAnn had watched an update on the mysterious disappearance of Mr. and Mrs. Clint Armstrong of Holden, Alberta. The couple had vanished, it seemed, while driving from Holden to visit their daughter in Peace River. MaryAnn pondered out loud, "How can a couple and their car disappear so completely without a trace?" Now Jake was wondering the same thing about his wife.

Although Jake was eager to inform the authorities of the situation and get as much help as possible, he didn't want a missing person's bulletin aired in the media until he had a chance to tell their extended family what was happening. That night, only a description of the car and its licence plate number were released to various news agencies.

Everything was moving at a whirlwind speed, and Jake felt like he was running to keep up with all the activity. He coped well, aided partly by his faith. But what Jake likely wasn't prepared for was an interrogation by the police. "There was a lot of speculation that her husband had done away with her," Edmonton Police Service inspector Joe Poss told the *Edmonton Journal* in an article printed 21 years after MaryAnn went missing. Retired detective Al Gowler added to the thought: "In just about any murder case that involves a family, the spouse is generally considered the prime suspect unless proven otherwise." In the early stages of the investigation, Jake was not only balancing worry and grief over the loss of his wife, but he also found himself accounting for his own actions over the 24 hours surrounding MaryAnn's disappearance. However, the suspicions surrounding Jake were soon squelched, and the police began looking for other suspects.

The police left the Plett home late the night MaryAnn disappeared, and Gail Cote and Hans Rissol, two of MaryAnn's colleagues who'd stayed with Jake during the police visit, left shortly afterwards. But it wasn't long before everyone reconvened. The police were anxious to see the area on the property that MaryAnn and Gail had staked out earlier. Even though the police asked Gail to meet them at 3:00 AM, Jake wanted to be there. Hans agreed to return to the Pletts' home and stay with the Pletts' two sons while Gail and Jake returned to the property. It took some time to find the small clearing surrounded by trees that Gail remembered measuring with MaryAnn. A steady drizzle compounded by the wind and the darkness of night added to the feeling of doom. Jake noticed what appeared to be fresh tire tracks, but they were difficult to distinguish because the rain had softened the earth.

If at that point Jake felt more destitute than he'd ever felt in his life, it was about to get worse. When Jake returned home, Lyndon and seven-year-old Nelson rushed their father and asked for their mother. Not long afterwards, Jake and MaryAnn's family members living in Edmonton convened in the Pletts' living room. They'd been alerted that something was wrong when neither Jake nor MaryAnn answered their own phone at 7:15 that morning. As honestly and calmly as possible, Jake explained the activities of the past night.

Now that the family was informed, Jake agreed that police could make the story public. Another search was being planned as he spoke, but he had an unsettled feeling in the pit of his stomach. Although he hoped for the best possible result— that MaryAnn would be found and brought home safe and sound—he was preparing himself for the worst. And although MaryAnn was officially listed as a missing person, the police were already concerned that the young woman had been murdered.

In his book, Jake described his feelings:

It was the beginning of the most difficult period of my life, which was to last much longer than I anticipated. It would involve many things and many people still unknown to me. What had begun as an ordinary day turned out to be a day that I will never forget, a day which changed my life-style [sic] and nearly shattered me. It was the day in which we stepped into the Valley of Shadows, where the darkness was almost overwhelming. ∾

FIRST DISCOVERY

Because MaryAnn was believed to have disappeared from the Looma-area acreage, Leduc RCMP were involved in the case from the beginning as the area was under their jurisdiction. They were putting most of their energy into scouring the acreage, combing it thoroughly in a shoulder-to-shoulder search with 16 constables and the assistance of police dogs and 33 Canadian Forces personnel from Namao, Alberta. They also pumped water out of a slough located on the property and examined its bottom for clues. Both efforts came up empty.

The city police focused their efforts on Edmonton. They, too, conducted a grid search, scouring streets and back lanes, contacting hotels and motels throughout the city looking for a "Mr. Cooper" and interviewing the four men they turned up with the same last name. When it came to finding any leads on MaryAnn or the mystery man, the city police came up empty. But on Friday, September 17, an employee at Don Wheaton Car Sales noticed a car on their lot that didn't appear to belong to the company. It didn't take long before they realized the car was the missing vehicle police were looking for.

By the time Jake learned of the discovery and headed to Don Wheaton, police were already at the scene, dusting for fingerprints and photographing the car from every angle. Jake noticed the radio dial was set for a station that MaryAnn didn't listen to and that the windshield wipers were turned on. After the car was towed to the police station, it was thoroughly vacuumed and the contents of each section emptied into separate bags and labelled; investigators were hoping these samples could give technicians some idea of where the car had been. Unfortunately, tests indicated that the samples weren't specific enough to suggest a particular geographic location where the car may have travelled.

Investigators quickly realized that whoever parked the car was prepared for the intense scrutiny—the vehicle had been wiped clean of fingerprints, and only two odd smudges of blood, one on the trunk latch and another on the rug in the trunk, had been missed. The blood was tested and determined to be the same type as MaryAnn's. Aside from MaryAnn's wig, found in the corner of the trunk, and a pair of sunglasses, which Jake told police didn't belong to him or to MaryAnn, the car was empty. There wasn't anything else, not a single piece of paper nor a discarded article of clothing, nothing, aside from the licence plate, number LN 54-07, to suggest that the 1970 Pontiac Laurentian belonged to the Pletts. Because so little concrete evidence was recovered, police were more inclined to elicit the public's help. They warned Jake that a string of prank calls and misleading information might follow, but that overall, public awareness might bring out important clues.

The prank calls and erroneous information tumbled into the police station without reservation. In some instances, a caller would identify himself or herself as a psychic and produce impressions on the case. One caller told police of seeing a domestic dispute take place along a rural roadway the day before MaryAnn's disappearance, and the caller was certain the couple was the missing woman and her husband arguing near a car that fit the description of the Pletts' vehicle. Jake denied the accusation and provided police with a detailed outline of what he and MaryAnn had done the day in question. Jake also agreed to take a polygraph test; he had no problems passing it.

By Thanksgiving weekend, the investigation appeared to have hit a dead end, and friends and family members were hoping to infuse it with new energy by organizing another search. Members of the church community that Jake and MaryAnn belonged to, members of the Real Estate Board, as well as friends, family members and the general public gathered to scour the area surrounding the Looma-area acreage. On October 11, 1971, Thanksgiving Monday, Jake and Corporal Stroud of the Leduc RCMP were first on the scene. Because no one had any idea how many volunteers would turn up for the search, only a dozen hand-drawn maps were available. It was rapidly obvious that wouldn't be enough. Almost 200 people showed up in 75 vehicles to do their part in searching a 32-kilometre radius around the Nelsons' acreage. Again, nothing concrete came of the search efforts.

Family friend Freda Wiebe suggested yet another approach to searching for information. She thought a mass mailing to rural residences around Looma might get people to thoroughly search their own properties. Such a project would be quite expensive; mailing the flyers alone would cost about $600, and Jake didn't have that kind of money. But Freda was persistent. She organized the entire mailout, donations and all. The flyer solicited the help of homeowners, reacquainting them with MaryAnn's story and asking them to carefully check their property.

The flyer also outlined all the items that Jake believed were in the car the day MaryAnn disappeared: a white Sunbeam electric can opener; two pairs of clip-on sunglasses in brown cases; one box of Kleenex; one green-blue plastic binder containing the car registration and warranty; and one plastic stacked picnic set. MaryAnn would have also most likely had her briefcase, a notebook, binders and business papers with her. A full description of MaryAnn and her car were also included in the flyer, along with the limited information they had about Mr. Cooper, and homeowners were encouraged to report anything they found that seemed out of the ordinary. The flyers were delivered by Friday, October 29. The kind efforts of a dear friend didn't yield the much hoped for results, though. It did, however, continue to raise public awareness, and that public awareness did bear fruit. ∾

A Second Discovery

On Saturday, October 30, two hunters in the Fort Assiniboine area, 129 kilometres north of Edmonton, were tracking game birds when they found a briefcase. James Boyd and Max Leingrand opened the case and knew right away to whom it belonged. They contacted Swan Hills RCMP, who immediately rushed to the scene. According to Jake, "the briefcase had been found behind three pines about 50 feet from the road, almost as though it had simply been thrown in from the roadway. The all-weather road led to the Pinto Creek Sawmill on Goose Lake, about 18 miles south and west of Fort Assiniboine."

A search of the area yielded more of MaryAnn's belongings, and everyone involved was hopeful they'd find the missing woman. Unfortunately, that time of year in Alberta usually means snow, and on November 5, winter hit, dropping 10 centimetres of snow. Searchers had to wait until spring to reconvene.

And although police did inform Jake of the discovery, investigators didn't want a curious public mulling about in the area and possibly destroying evidence, so he was sworn to secrecy until a body was found. It proved to be a long winter.

On Friday, April 14, employees from the Pinto Creek Sawmill discovered women's clothing while working on a drainage ditch. Three days later, Jake confirmed the clothing belonged to his wife, and on Wednesday, April 19, the partial remains of MaryAnn Plett were uncovered in the same, densely wooded area that detective Gowler would later say suggested the killer definitely was familiar with the area.

At 7:00 PM, Jake arrived at the RCMP station, needing to see for himself that he'd finally reached the end of his terrifying ordeal. Animals and rodents had devoured much of MaryAnn's body. All that remained was the top part of her skull, a piece of femur and another unidentified bone fragment—there was no way that Jake could visually identify his wife. But he was sure it was MaryAnn. Their family dentist, Dr. John Woytuck of Sherwood Park, confirmed what Jake already knew. What they couldn't tell by the remains was how MaryAnn had died or whether she had been sexually assaulted. What they did know was that Jake now had a funeral to prepare for, and the police knew, without a doubt, they were dealing with a murder.

It may have been the first time since September 17, 1971, when MaryAnn initially went missing, that everyone was well aware of what was expected of them. For Jake, processing his emotions and understanding what his new reality meant was partially dealt with by holding a funeral service, organizing memorial donations to Gideons International and arranging to distribute the more than 300 Bibles that made their way into hotels, motels and schools. The donations helped him deal with the grief of losing his wife and gave him the strength to guide his two sons through their grieving process.

Jake also began speaking at churches, sharing how his faith in God had guided him through the most terrifying time of his life. And his writing and publication of *Valley of Shadows* succeeded in keeping MaryAnn's story in the public eye. He even met another woman: Marion Craggs, a woman from the church Jake attended, showed up at the family's doorstep on May 1, 1972, offering her help in writing thank-you notes to everyone who had donated to the Gideons in MaryAnn's memory. Marion and Jake hit it off from the moment they met, and the couple married on August 12 of that same year.

Progression through the investigation was considerably slower than what happened in Jake's personal life. Despite the countless tips that poured into the RCMP and Edmonton City Police, the elusive Mr. Cooper was never identified. The closest they came to any clue about the man was shortly after MaryAnn's disappearance, when another female realtor reported receiving a call from a Dave Cooper. She described the man as being "a real talker...in a real hurry," and he said he was from "the east." The woman wasn't able to show him the property he wanted to see that night, as her appointment schedule was fully booked. It appears she never heard from the man again.

Another key part of the investigation that never seemed to be ironed out was motive. Why was MaryAnn targeted in the first place? She had no enemies; anyone who knew her would attest to that fact. Was the man a sexual predator looking to take advantage of a kind and trusting woman? If sex was the motive, why weren't there other, similar crimes at that time in Alberta, where MaryAnn's abduction and murder took place, or elsewhere in Canada? Or was this predator simply a mentally unbalanced individual playing a sick game of cat and mouse with no other motive than to capture his prey and get away with murder?

Because Cooper left no personal information with MaryAnn, everything about the man was speculation. Because each visit began with a prearranged meeting at Bonnie Doon Mall, was it possible Cooper had targeted MaryAnn because he lived in that area and she had advertised the Looma-area acreage by describing its distance from the shopping centre? Or was it a more sinister motive? Was it possible, as her son Nelson suggested years later, that MaryAnn was targeted because she was a woman working in a man's world? Could the entire situation have been orchestrated out of jealousy?

During his involvement with the case, Gowler said they "never had any hard and fast leads." Still, investigators were hopeful that they'd eventually find MaryAnn's killer. Jake was equally hopeful. In his book, Jake shared his dream of one day answering the phone or a knock on the door to find an investigator telling him what he so longed to hear—that they had found Mr. Cooper.

Sadly, Jake would never hear those words in this lifetime. On February 11, 1978, Jake and his second wife Marion were killed when the Western Airlines jet they were flying in crashed near Cranbrook, BC. They left behind their sons, Lyndon and Nelson, and a baby girl named Carlene, who would have celebrated her fourth birthday with her parents just nine days later. ∾

THE LAST WORD

Lindsay Buziak and MaryAnn Plett were two women with a promising future who were only doing their jobs, both struck down in the prime of their life.

No matter how tenuous, hope reigns eternal. For the Plett children and their extended families, a desire to see justice in the death of their loved one continues. As Jake wrote, appealing to his reading public in *Valley of Shadows*, "Someone must have known [Cooper]…I appeal to the conscience of anyone who might be withholding such information. Please come forward and make it known."

Lindsay Buziak's family is no doubt hoping for a much quicker answer to the question of who killed her.

In February 2009, police released a composite sketch of a woman suspected of seeing Lindsay on the day she was murdered. The sketch was developed through the testimony provided by witnesses. The Caucasian woman with short, blonde hair was described as between 35 and 45 years of age, neatly dressed in what appeared to be a black designer dress or skirt with red and white stripes. These witnesses also described a similarly well-dressed, tall, dark-haired, Caucasian male.

Police also removed any suspicion surrounding Lindsay's boyfriend, Jason Zailo, saying he was not a suspect in the case.

As of this writing, police are still looking for Lindsay's murderer.

Chapter Nine

Obscure Cases Still Haunt Investigators

F or one reason or another, information surrounding an unsolved murder can be particularly scarce. Sometimes the police choose to withhold information for investigative purposes. At other times, it's because there's not much information available to share. This happens to be the case in a recent double murder involving the son of an acquaintance of mine and his business partner. This young man's family is desperate for answers and anxious to learn more about why, when and by whom their loved one was killed, but even they aren't able to extract anything but the most basic information from the police so as not to jeopardize the inquiry into the murder of this man and his colleague. Sadly, this means the media doesn't cover these stories as thoroughly as others and, therefore, the public isn't aware of these cases.

On the other hand, some police departments spend considerable time and money in updating websites with information on cold cases in their area, anxious for the public's assistance in their quest to flesh out whatever evidence they might have on a particular case. Sometimes officers might have little more than a photograph and the date, place and method of a murder. Sometimes they have even less than that, and a plea to the public might be the only hope for progress. What follows is an assortment of cases in which little is known about the murder or limited information was revealed to the public. ❧

DOES MONEY TALK?

Forty-five year old Susan Tice was a woman with a career she loved, four children to be proud of and a new lease on life. She was recently divorced and looking forward to a fresh start, having moved across the country, from Calgary to Toronto, to do so. The social worker had recently set down roots in her new city of choice on July 9, 1983.

Susan would never see the leaves turn in famous Cabbagetown or get her fill of Toronto's skyline at night. On August 17 of the same year, just five and a half weeks after arriving in the big TO and settling into her Grace Street home, Susan was dead. Murdered in an upstairs bedroom. When her family was not able to get in touch with her, they called another relative and asked if she was okay. That individual would have been alerted that something was wrong as soon as they entered her house and found it ransacked. This relative found Susan lying in a pool of her own blood, her body peppered with stab wounds.

Violent crime, even murder, isn't as shocking in a city the size of Toronto as it would be in a small, quaint, country village. But because police couldn't seem to hone in on a suspect, the homicide was troubling to residents and investigators alike. Susan hadn't been in town long enough to make any enemies or to develop a relationship that could have soured. She wasn't even in town long enough for a secret admirer to feel jilted and lash out at the woman in anger. There seemed no motive for her murder, and without a motive, suspects are usually scarce.

Time dims memory, even when it comes to murder, but the story of this seemingly random, unsolved slaying would resurface when the city faced another brutal stabbing. This time the victim wasn't an unknown, middle-aged, career woman living on her own. It was a fresh-faced 22-year-old from a notable Toronto family.

Erin Gilmour had led what some might call a charmed life. As Max Haines pointed out in his story "Four Strangers in Life, They Were United in Death," she was well schooled, having attended such elite institutions as Campion School in Athens, Greece, and the Lycée Française de Los Angeles. Erin later attended the University of Western Ontario.

In October 1983, she spread her wings again, moving out of the home she shared with her mother and taking an apartment on Hazelton Avenue in Toronto. She didn't have long to enjoy her newfound independence. On the evening of December 20, 24-year-old Anthony Monk called on Erin and found her apartment door slightly ajar. It was strange to be sure, foolish even. This was the big city, after all.

Anthony pushed the door open a little more and called out for Erin. When she didn't bounce out to meet him, Anthony thought perhaps she'd been delayed at work. The boutique where Erin worked was just steps away, so he walked to the store, only to find the shop closed for the day, the lights turned down and the doors locked.

Surely his heart must have been throbbing, his blood pressure rising, and the thought slowly taking hold that something was definitely wrong as he made his way back to Erin's apartment. This time he went inside; he went all the way into the master bedroom before he found her. Like Susan Tice earlier that summer, Erin had been brutally stabbed to death; one news report also suggested she was raped.

When the police retraced Erin's steps and compared it to Anthony's rendition of the events of that night, it appeared the young woman was killed sometime between leaving work that evening, around 8:45 PM, and before Anthony arrived at her apartment the first time, at around 9:30 PM. Did Erin leave her door open in anticipation of Anthony's visit, and a demented stranger happened along and took advantage of the situation?

Or was her attack preplanned; was she the victim of a silent suitor?

Again, investigators had no leads and no suspects. The police did have a hunch, however. Although it's never enough to put a criminal behind bars, sometimes a hunch pays off. Toronto police noticed the method of murder used in the death of Susan Tice in August, in particular the multiple stabbings, bore a striking similarity to the Erin Gilmour homicide. The two victims lived a scant four kilometres from each other. And like the Tice killing, there were no solid leads or suspects in Erin's murder.

There was, however, DNA. And in 2000, the DNA retrieved from the two crimes was tested in new, updated, high-tech facilities, and the results confirmed that the same person killed both women. Now it was a matter of matching the results from the tested DNA to a suspect. That, however, is where investigators were stymied. They still needed to identify a solid suspect in either case. And it's not like the police hadn't been digging. According to a Sun Media news report in November 2008, an estimated 4500 people have been considered as possible suspects in the two murders over the years, but police are still searching for the killer.

In 2008, police decided to entice possible witnesses with a reward of up to $50,000 for information leading to the arrest of the person responsible for prematurely ending the lives of Susan Tice and Erin Gilmour. Investigators believe the killer lived or worked in the area and was likely between 18 and

35 years old at the time of the murders. That would make the perpetrator in his late 40s to early 60s today. Their cases might have grown cold long ago, but these women haven't been forgotten by their families or by the police. ❧

MISSING, MURDERED AND NAMELESS

In every murder plot, fiction or non-fiction, there are usually three main motivators in the commission of a homicide: sex, greed and power. Very few situations get the ire up like love gone sour or a sneaky or unfaithful partner. Most of us appreciate the value of a dollar, but some less-savoury individuals will stop at nothing to stuff their pockets. And then there's the burning desire for power and control; perhaps someone stands in the way of professional advancement and a murderer believes the only way to climb the corporate ladder and assume what they believe to be their rightful position at the top is by eliminating the competition. Yet a few murders are so grizzly, so over the top, that how these primary factors work together to form the possible reason behind a particular homicide baffles even the most imaginative of investigative minds.

Such is the case with a story out of north-central Alberta.

It was the spring of 1977. A couple was picking up a pump at a property near Tofield, Alberta, when they made a discovery worthy of a Quentin Tarantino movie plot. Tucked under a pile of limestone inside a septic tank, there appeared to be an oddly shaped mass that ever so slightly resembled a human body. Had it occurred to the couple that it was April 1, they might not have investigated their discovery, thinking it a cruel hoax.

On closer observation, it became clear that this was no April Fool's prank—what the couple had discovered was indeed a dead body, and whoever was responsible for the murder of this John Doe, soon to be nicknamed "Septic Tank Sam," was so filled with rage that he was blinded by it, driven by its force, and went into overdrive when attacking the man who was, on his discovery, little more than a melted mass of flesh. In fact, Septic Tank Sam's body was so completely brutalized it took some time to determine if the body belonged to a man or a woman. The victim in question had been shot but was still very much alive when he was tortured to death by a blowtorch. Clearly the killer wanted to do more than simply murder the man: he wanted to sear his message home.

It's hard to imagine the motivation behind the murder of this individual, who today, more than 30 years after his death, remains a nameless corpse. Since it was quite conceivable that the body could have remained there indefinitely, decaying and being consumed by pests and rodents until there was nothing left but a scattering of unidentifiable bone shards, Septic Tank Sam's murder could have gone undiscovered. The man could have died and no one would have ever known.

The discovery of his body before it was totally consumed, decomposed and scattered was little less than a miracle. And yet this discovery has done little more than land the victim in a cold case file at Tofield's RCMP detachment. The unearthing of his body hasn't led to a single clue in the case. No one knows who killed him, why he was murdered, exactly when he was murdered or if he was killed at the location where his body was discovered or somewhere else.

There are theories, however. An article dated September 3, 2007, suggests theories surrounding gangs and illegal substances and the possibility that "Sam was a transient who may have gotten into trouble over drugs." The idea isn't without its merit. Most families have a black sheep somewhere in their family tree, and a young man frustrated and angry and searching to fill a void can easily fall victim to the seamier side of life. And because, according to some sources, rural areas surrounding Alberta's two largest cities were used in several instances as a dumping ground for bodies in the 1970s, it's quite conceivable that Septic Tank Sam meets the profile as one of these victims.

On the other hand, the clothing recovered at the scene— a blue work shirt, T-shirt, blue jeans, grey wool socks, imitation Wallabee shoes—suggest the victim could have been a labourer who might have been passing through Alberta, attracted by the possibility of a career in the oil fields and looking for work.

There have been several newspaper articles over the years recounting Septic Tank Sam's sad story and appealing to the public for information, and according to one source, the RCMP are typically contacted once or twice a year by individuals looking for a missing family member. Maybe they have somehow heard of the case of Septic Tank Sam or perhaps they saw a photo of the facial reconstruction and computer-generated image developed over the years and thought the image bore a resemblance to a long-lost relative. Advances in DNA technology have made it possible to identify an individual when a family member shows up and provides a comparative sample. "We run down every one of those leads," Sergeant Jim Warren told reporters in September 2007, adding that identifying Septic Tank Sam "is key in finding the killer."

So far, no positive identification has been made. ∞

JUST MAKING A FEW BUCKS

Learning to earn a wage and balance a bank account are basics most youngsters tackle with rigour and excitement on their journey to adulthood. They learn that money means purchasing power, the ability to add a little flexibility and freedom to their lives and the chance to plan for an exciting future.

In large city centres, employment options for youth are considerably more plentiful than those in smaller communities such as Standard, Alberta. With a 2008 population of 380— give or take a few boomerang babies coming home to nest now and again—the community, located about 90 kilometres from Calgary, is a wholesome place to raise a family. Everyone knows each other. Families look out for each other's kids, residents have a genuine feeling of goodwill, and for many it is a safe place to call home. A website outlining the community's profile boasts that in this town, "crime statistics are substantially lower in the region than typical of larger metropolitan centres like the City of Calgary."

There are problems, however. Part-time jobs are practically non-existent, and the few babysitting jobs that come up now and again don't employ anywhere near the number of potential babysitters available. So when 15-year-old Kelly Cook received a call at 8:30 AM on Wednesday, April 22, asking if she was available to babysit for a man named Bill Christensen, she jumped at the chance, even though she'd never heard the man's name before. Still, he said he lived there. Kelly, young and trusting, wouldn't have thought twice about checking him out, especially since he'd likely told her he got her name and phone number from a friend of hers who Bill had called with the same request. Kelly's friend wasn't able to take the job, so she gave him Kelly's name.

As Kelly got ready to fly out the door at 8:30 that night, she bumped into her dad, who was just getting home from work. Walter remembered his daughter said hello, told him she was going babysitting and rushed out the door. The last Walter saw of his daughter she was driving away in what was later described as a "full-sized North American car." There was a man in the driver's seat, to be sure, but neither Walter nor his wife, Marion, got a good look at him.

Like most families, the Cooks had a system. Whenever Kelly went babysitting, she'd always call home as soon as she arrived at her destination. Within an hour of her departure, Marion knew something was wrong. Kelly hadn't called home. By then, Marion was on the phone, asking everyone they knew if they'd seen Kelly or if they knew of any new people who'd moved into the area. No one had. Not even the local postmistress.

By now it was almost 10:00 PM. The phone rang; a call was being patched through from a pay phone in Hussar, another small community about 25 kilometres east of Standard on Highway 561. There were no words; only the sounds of a female screaming. It wasn't clear if the call came from Kelly or not, but it didn't seem likely the Cooks would receive such a phone call at that particular moment in time, given the circumstances. The Cooks now believed their daughter was in trouble. The reality left them feeling helpless and impotent.

Police were called in, and because of the circumstances surrounding Kelly's absence, they were immediately concerned. Search parties manned by police and volunteers were established, and the area around Standard was thoroughly combed. "Those days, I carried a shotgun around with me while we were searching, and if I'd have found him, I would have shot him," Walter confided to Dave Breakenridge of the *Calgary Sun* in a follow-up article, published in November 2005, nearly 25 years after Kelly's abduction.

On June 28, 1981, Kelly's lifeless body was discovered in the Chin Lake Reservoir, east of Lethbridge and a good hour or more south of her Standard home. She was still clothed, and her body had been "tied to cinder blocks and tossed into the water." Calgary RCMP corporal Andy Johnson told Breakenridge that Kelly's body was "in an advanced state of decomposition and there was no obvious cause of death."

Investigation into the case revealed that Kelly wasn't likely the originally intended target. It appeared a man had been trying to track down a young girl whose photograph appeared in the local paper a couple of months earlier. The unknown man had called the local school principal, asking for her name and phone number, and although the principal refused to provide the information, the mystery man somehow managed to track it down for himself. The man in question did contact the girl, and she, too, was asked if she could babysit. But she was unavailable, so she gave the man Kelly's name as an alternative for the night in question.

The man calling himself Bill Christensen was described as a heavy-set man about 5 feet 10 inches in height, somewhere between 30 and 45 years of age, with "brown hair, a square face, wide nose and sideburns." Walter and Marion Cook still hope their daughter's killer will be discovered, and a reward of $100,000 was established for information leading to the arrest and conviction of Kelly's killer. ❧

IN THE LINE OF DUTY

Every year, peace officers in Canada lose their lives for simply doing their jobs. Some die accidentally, victims of highway accidents, for example. Others, however, are gunned down, murdered in cold blood while chasing or apprehending a suspect. Between 1879 and 1994, 227 police officers were killed in the line of duty. In 1994, Prime Minister Jean Chretien unveiled a granite memorial on Parliament grounds honouring the selfless commitment of these brave peacekeepers. And in April 2009, Sergeant Steve Gibson started out on the third annual "drive to remember," motoring the more than 5000 miles from BC, throughout the U.S. and into Washington, DC, raising awareness about the 141 police officers killed on the job in Canada and the U.S. in 2008 alone.

Theirs is a dangerous job—one that can sometimes lead to murder.

Thirty-nine-year-old Arthur Duncan wasn't likely expecting much action while he was walking his beat during the early morning hours of July 2, 1917. Calgary was a budding city, and with a constant flow of new residents, it wasn't uncommon for a beat cop to have to break up a drunken brawl or two. Then again, it wasn't exactly the Wild West. This was a civilized, peaceful city. Duncan was also an experienced officer. He'd served on the force in Scotland for 12 years before becoming an officer in Calgary in 1911. He knew his job well, and that day started out as routinely as most others.

Working the graveyard shift sometimes meant a long, slow shift. That's likely what the good constable was expecting. Duncan had reported in at the station at midnight, and then continued on his rounds. But when he didn't check in at 1:00 AM, and then missed his 2:00 AM report, his sergeant started to worry. Duncan was a reliable officer. He wouldn't skip two checks. His colleagues set out to look for him.

At 4:40 that morning, a resident found Duncan near the corner of 8 Avenue and 8 Street SW. He was dead. Killed by two of four bullets fired from what was determined to be a Colt .45 pistol. One bullet hit him in the jaw, the other in the chest. Both bullets passed through his lungs. Chief Alfred Cuddy said, in a letter to Duncan's family, that the coroner's findings suggested Duncan didn't suffer. He likely died instantly and didn't even know he'd been shot.

During their investigation, police pieced together Duncan's last moments. According to a *Calgary Sun* article reviewing the case in November 2005, police believe Duncan "stumbled upon a burglar or burglars trying to stash or recover stolen property from a space underneath the Revelstoke Sawmills Co. building." The perpetrators likely noticed Duncan before he clued into what they were doing.

A scattered assortment of witnesses came forward, testifying to what they'd seen around the time Duncan was killed. One gave evidence of a soldier walking away from the scene, kit bag in hand. He was described as about 5 feet 10 inches in height, weighing about 165 pounds, "with fair hair, wearing a light-coloured suit and cap." Over time, this phantom soldier earned a reputation as a seasoned criminal who'd already had at least one encounter with the law, but whoever he was, the man was never named or apprehended and remained little more than a ghostly image in the public's mind.

Police also considered another scenario: if the gun used in the crime wasn't an army service revolver, which was quite possible if the unknown soldier passing by hadn't had anything to do with Duncan's homicide, the murder weapon could have been purchased from a neighbourhood pawn shop. If this was the case, the suspect list could include almost anyone.

It's unclear if the police ever really had a solid lead in the case, or if their efforts were based solely on speculation, but officers across the country were informed of the murder of one of their own. Newspapers carried the story, often describing Duncan's killer as a "habitual criminal and a desperate man." The investigation even branched into the U.S. At times, police grasped at whatever opportunities they could, checking out anyone who matched the only description they had and crossing possible suspects off their list, one at a time. A $1000 award was posted for information leading to the arrest and conviction of Duncan's killer. Still, the case continued to frustrate the police.

Today, nine decades after the fact, Duncan's killer has never been brought to justice. He remains one of only 11 members of the Calgary Police Service to have been shot dead.

Duncan's murder has the dubious honour of being named the first murder of a police officer in Calgary and the "oldest cold case" in the city.

Notes on Sources

Chapter One: Dana Bradley

Canadian Press. "Murder Trail Turns Warmer." April 18, 1991.

CBC News. "David Somerton holed up in Calgary; SWAT team called in." August 27, 1999.

—. "Malcom Cuff charged with long-unsolved murder." December 20, 2000.

—. "Newfoundland court OKs plea bargain in girl's death." February 13, 2003.

—. "Dana Bradley's murder investigation 'active' after 25 years: Police." December 14, 2006.

CTV News special. "The ghost of Dana Bradley." January 16, 2003.

CTV News special. "A singer's tribute to Dana Bradley." December 6, 2002.

Dooley, Danette. "Where are they now? Police still probing unsolved missing persons cases." *The Telegram* (St. John's), November 29, 2004.

Harris, Mike. "Every morning before I start work, I look at her." Editorial in the *Toronto Sun*, May 25, 1999.

Jackson, Craig. "Somerton quizzed about Carroll murder." *The Telegram* (St. John's), March 10, 1999.

—. "Bradley case is still open" and "Case still unsolved." *The Telegram* (St. John's), December 10, 2006.

Kean, Gary. "Durnford soon eligible for full parole." *The Western Star,* January 14, 2008.

McGrath, Darrin. *Hitching a Ride: The Unsolved Murder of Dana Bradley.* St. John's, NL: Flanker Press Ltd., 2003.

Chapter Two: Sharron Prior

McNamara, Michelle. True Crime Diary, "Sharron's Story," published March 28, 2008, http://truecrimediary.com/index.cfm?page=cases&id=49

http://coolopolis.blogspot.com/2008/02/who-was-chateauguay-sex-killer.html

http://en.wikipedia.org/wiki/Off-island_suburbs#Off-island_suburbs

http://www.Québecheritageweb.com/trail/trail_details.aspx?&trailId=33

http://www.sharronprior.com

Chapter Three: Theresa Allore

Abercrombie, Bill, with the Alberta Trapper's Association.

Allore, John. "Bad dream house," personal blog, http://baddreamhouse.blogspot.com/

CTV News, "Who killed Theresa?" News special updated March 14, 2005.

Hanes, Allison. "Who killed Theresa Allore?" *National Post* serial, June 16, 2006.

Rossmo, D. Kim. *Criminal Investigative Failures.* Boca Raton, FL: CRC Press, Taylor & Francis Group, 2009.

http://www.whokilledtheresa.com/

Chapter Four: Candace Derksen

Canadian Press. "Murder charge laid in 23-year-old case" and "Charge laid in Winnipeg cold case: Suspect deemed 'sexually deviant.'" May 17, 2007.

CBC News staff. "Arrest made in 1984 killing of Winnipeg teen." May 16, 2007.

—. "Winnipeggers 'elated' by arrest in 1984 death of teen." May 17, 2007.

Derksen, Wilma. *Have You Seen Candace?* Wheaton, IL: Living Books (Tyndale House Publishers Inc.) 1991.

"DNA leads to arrest in 1984 Winnipeg 'cold case.'" CTV.ca, May 16, 2007.

McIntyre, Mike. "Man accused in the murder of Candace Derksen wants bail." *Winnipeg Free Press,* October 31, 2007.

Sun Media articles: March 26, 1992, March 5, 12, 2001, November 3, 2002, January 16, 2005, May 16–17, 2007.

Winnipeg Police Service Media Release. "Project 'Angel' leads to arrest in 1984 Candace Derksen homicide." May 16, 2007.

http://www.winnipegfirst.ca/article/2007/05/16/mother_hasnt_really_forgiven

Chapter Five: Alexandra Wiwcharuk

Bernhardt, Darren. "Saskatoon murder remains unsolved." Saskatchewan News Network, 2008.

—. "Killer may yet be found in 46-year-old unsolved murder." *Edmonton Journal.*

Butala, Sharon. *The Girl in Saskatoon.* Toronto, ON: HarperCollins Publishers Ltd., 2008.

The StarPhoenix articles: June 2, 4, 6, 1962; May 16, 1992; January 10, 2004; June 25 and October 1, 2008.

http://www.cbc.ca/fifth/2008-2009/the_girl_in_saskatoon/video.html

http://cnews.canoe.ca/CNEWS/Canada/2009/03/05/8638126-cp.html

http://www.edmontonjournal.com/news/Maclean+dubs+Saskatoon+Canada+crime+capital/1360127/story.html

Chapter Six: Charles Horvath

Various news agencies contributed endless articles and produced several news documentaries on the Horvath case: CHBC TV, Kelowna Crime Stoppers, *Banff Crag & Canyon*, *B.C. Report*, *Britain's Woman Magazine*, *Calgary Sun*, *Cambridge Evening News*, *The Daily Courier (Kelowna)*, *The Evening Courier* (Halifax, Britain), *The Gazette* (Montreal), *The Hamilton Spectator*, *Hello!* (London, England), *The Independent* (London), *The International Express* (Canadian edition), *Kelowna Capital News*, *ME* (British magazine), *Missing Treasures*, *Okanagan Today*, *The Province* (Vancouver), *The Mail* (Halifax, Britain), *The People*, *South China Post*, *The Sunday Mirror*, *The Telegraph & Argus*, *Today*, *The Toronto Star*, *Yorkshire Post*, *Unsolved Mysteries*, *The Vancouver Sun*, *The Winnipeg Sun*.

Chapter Seven: Tanya Van Cuylenborg and Jay Roland Cook

Barber, Mike. "Part 5: Serial killers—they're not always who we think." *Seattle Post-Intelligencer*, February 21, 2003.

Hefley, Diana. "Young couple's slayings confounds detective." HeraldNet.com, December 14, 2008.

—. "Recent tip in 1978 slayings brings hope of resolution." HeraldNet.com, January 18, 2009.

Michaud, Stephen G., and Hugh Aynesworth. *Murderers Among Us*. Signet Books. 1991.

Skagit Valley Herald articles: November 25, 27, 28 and 30, 1987.

Snohomish County Sheriff's Office Cold Case Cards. http://sheriff.snoco.org/Sheriff_Services/MissingPersons/Cards.htm

Unsolved Mysteries. "A young couple's vacation ends in rape and murder." http://www.unsolved.com/ajaxfiles/mur_jay_cook_tanya_van_cuylenborg.htm

http://www.alternet.org/blogs/reproductivejustice/100860/when_men_murder_women:_new_report_details_homicide_rates/

Chapter Eight: Lindsay Buziak and MaryAnn Plett

Lindsay Buziak

"B.C. realtor stabbed multiple times: Autopsy." CTV.ca, February 5, 2008.

Clarke, Brennan. "Father makes emotional plea to killer at funeral for real estate agent." *Globe and Mail,* February 11, 2008.

Hunter, Justine, and Murray Langdon. "Slain agent was 'targeted' colleague says." *Globe and Mail,* February 5, 2008.

"Lindsay Buziak Murder Investigation." http://www.saanichpolice.ca/crimewatch/media/08_2682update6.html

Moreau, Vivian. "Updated: One year after Lindsay Buziak's murder, police have yet to make arrests." *Saanich News,* January 30, 2009.

"Sketch helps spark tips in Buziak case." *Goldstream Gazette,* February 19, 2009.

Thomas, Nicki. "Victoria realtor attack eerily similar." Sun Media, February 7, 2008.

Times Colonist articles on Lindsay Buziak: February 4, 7, 2008; February 1, 3, 2009.

MaryAnn Plett

"42nd body found at site of crash of PWA aircraft." *Globe and Mail,* February 14, 1978.

"Aircrew recordings destroyed by crash," *Globe and Mail,* February 15, 1978.

Golbeck, Wilfred. "The mystery of MaryAnn Plett." *Edmonton Journal,* October 25, 1992.

Lawley, Const. Ryan. "Near-perfect murder can be solved with the right lead, plus advances in forensics." *Edmonton Sun,* September 15, 2003.

Plett, Jake. *Valley of Shadows.* Beaverlodge, AB: Horizon House Publishers, 1975.

Smith, Barbara. *Deadly Encounters: True Crime Stories of Alberta.* Toronto, ON: Hounslow Press (Dundurn Press Ltd.), 1993.

Chapter Nine: Obscure Cases Still Haunt Investigators

Susan Tice and Erin Gilmour

Haines, Max. "Four strangers in life, they were united in death." Sun Media. October 15, 1989.

Sun Media articles: February 3, 2000; August 27, 2003; September 21, 2004; November 18, 2008.

Septic Tank Sam

Kauth, Glenn. "Cold case still being chased." Sun Media. September 3, 2007.

http://www.albertamissingpersons.ca/images/stories/library/data_files/7690-77.pdf

http://www.torontopolice.on.ca/homicide/case/6

Kelly Cook

Breakenridge, Dave. "Who killed Kelly?" *Calgary Sun,* November 5, 2005.

Calgary RCMP General Investigation Section information bulletin.

http://www.albertafirst.com/profiles/statspack/20582.html

Arthur Duncan

Breakenridge, Dave. "He never had a chance." *Calgary Sun,* November 9, 2005.

www.calgarypolice.ca

General Website Sources

http://blogs.dallasobserver.com/unfairpark/2009/05/early_this_morning_a_canadian.php

http://www.cacp.ca/memorial/index/history (Canadian Association of Chiefs of Police)

http://www.cbc.ca/news/background/rcmp/inthelineofduty.html

http://www.mcsc.ca/Statistics.aspx (Missing Children Society of Canada)

http://www.statcan.gc.ca/daily-quotidien/070718/dq070718b-eng.htm (Statistics Canada)

http://www.statcan.gc.ca/daily-quotidien/080717/dq080717b-eng.htm

http://www.statcan.gc.ca/daily-quotidien/081023/dq081023a-eng.htm

About the Author

Lisa Wojna

Lisa Wojna, author of several other non-fiction books, has worked in the community newspaper industry as a writer and journalist and has travelled all over Canada, from the windy prairies of Manitoba to northern British Columbia, and even to the wilds of Africa. Although writing and photography have been a central part of her life for as long as she can remember, it's the people behind every story that are her motivation and give her the most fulfillment.

Check out more True Crime from

QUAGMIRE
PRESS

AVAILABLE DECEMBER 2009
CANADIAN CON ARTISTS
by Lisa Wojna

Con artists everywhere exploit human virtues—trust, hope, compassion—and twist them into weaknesses, all in the hopes of making a quick buck. From cons who misrepresent and misguide to those who just downright lie, read about some of Canada's most convincing con men.

$18.95 • ISBN: 978-1-926695-06-8 • 5.25" x 8.25" • 256 pages

DEADLY CANADIAN WOMEN
The Stories Behind the Crimes of Canada's Most Notorious Women
by Patricia MacQuarrie

When we think of a killer, most of us don't think of a woman. But these Canadian women did the unthinkable and murdered their spouses, their lovers, their children or even complete strangers.

$18.95 • ISBN: 978-0-9783409-2-6 • 5.25" x 8.25" • 256 pages

MISSING!
The Disappeared, Lost or Abducted in Canada
by Lisa Wojna

The people in this book have one thing in common—they all vanished, many without a trace. From BC's infamous highway of tears to the Robert Pickton trial, read the stories of the disappeared and lost in Canada.

$18.95 • ISBN: 978-0-9783409-0-2 • 5.25" x 8.25" • 264 pages

Available from your local bookseller or by contacting the
distributor,
Lone Pine Publishing
1-800-661-9017
www.lonepinepublishing.com